WE'RE THERE
FOR YOU, BABY

WE'RE THERE
FOR YOU, BABY

THE ENTREPRENEUR'S GUIDE
TO THE GALAXY

VOL. 2

BARBARA BRY & NEIL SENTURIA

blackbird
VENTURES

LA JOLLA, CALIFORNIA

Published by Blackbird Ventures
2223 Avenida de la Playa
Suite 206
La Jolla, CA 92037
www.imthereforyoubaby.com
baby@imthereforyoubaby.com
(858) 754-3201

Publishing Consulting and Product Development::
BookStudio, LLC, www.bookstudiobooks.com

Cover Design: John R. McCulley, McCulley Design Lab, www.mcculleydesign.com
Book Design: Charles McStravick
Author Photo: Brent Haywood

PRINTED IN THE UNITED STATES OF AMERICA

TO OUR GREATEST START-UPS,
SARAH, RACHEL, RACHEL AND ETHAN

CONTENTS

INTRODUCTION

Today, everyone needs to think like an entrepreneur whether you work in your own business, a large company, a non-profit organization or government.

The life of an entrepreneur is filled with ups and down, successes and failures. Barbara and I have experienced both. While failures are stressful, they often have led to exciting new opportunities—such as the weekly column that we started writing in August 2011 for *U-T San Diego*.

The story of how this came to pass began in August 2008 when we invested in an online news company that we thought could be the future of local news in San Diego and around the United States.

Rule #500:
When blinded by the light, get very dark sunglasses,
go see your opthamologist and look again.

We hired writers and made partnering deals. We were filled with ourselves, we were rolling and then something unlikely happened. That is why one of my most favorite books is "The Black Swan," by Nassim Taleb. On September 15, 2008, Lehman Brothers, the powerhouse investment bank, went broke.

And so here we had backed this little company in the midst of one of the largest financial debacles in history. You try to raise money for an underfunded, interesting, but unprofitable, still unproven company in the late fall of 2008. By April 2009, the stock market had tumbled—the Dow had dropped from 10,000 to 6600. There was blood in the streets, terror in the windows of Wall Street, and our little company was trying to keep its head above water, while the outgoing tide was trying to take us to Australia.

I will not recount here the complete tale of woe. We tried hard, perhaps harder than we had ever worked for any of the companies that we have been involved in. We were sad about our inability to make the idea work and have a life. (During the same period, AOL managed to spend $200 million on Patch, its little online local news adventure, with the same economic result.)

Finally in the summer of 2010, we closed up. There is always some limited honor in embracing reality.

So it is now the summer 2010. Barbara picks up the pieces and presses on with her life focused on involvement in the community. Meanwhile, I enter the interim suicide watch, because I know, I am sure, that I will never get a job in this town again, ever again. I am done, toast, finished, relegated to the trash heap of guys who broke their pick and died on the mountain, while others behind me, just come along and walk over my bones. I will never be a CEO again. I will never raise another dime. I am a shadow.

So I decide to become a consultant.

The first thing I do is call a consultant who tells me that if you want to be a consultant, you have to have a book. I decide that if

I need a book, then I am going to write one that tries to tell the truth of the entrepreneurial adventure—not the glossy, I made no mistakes, I got funding and then I sold for a billion dollars—not that book. But rather a book with a few more gory details about how the sausage actually gets made.

Remember, I had labored in Hollywood for 10 years, so I figured I could write a book. I did a quick calculation that a 220-page book needed approximately 62,000 words, so from June 2010 to September 2010, I sat down and wrote the book, *I'm There for You Baby: The Entrepreneur's Guide to the Galaxy.*

And during that summer, I also tried to get work as a consultant.

No one would hire me. They sensed that beneath my benign exterior, anxious to quietly help and offer calm, reasoned advice, lurked an unfulfilled CEO in waiting, whose DNA did not easily make minor suggestions.

A consultant gets in the back seat of the car and asks questions like: Where do we want to go? How do you propose we might consider the various routes to get there? In contrast, a CEO gets in the front seat, and right after the client puts the key in the ignition, tells him he is doing it all wrong, takes the wheel, and says I know exactly how to get there—and floors it.

After I finish the book, we sent it to Jeff Light, the editor at *U-T San Diego,* to see if the paper would review it. Jeff read the book and invited us to lunch during which he invited us to write a column on entrepreneurship. (The *U-T* never reviewed the book!)

Now remember that Barbara Bry, my bride, had been a real, professional journalist. She had been a business writer for *The Sacramento Bee* and *The Los Angeles Times.* She has an MBA from Harvard (why she married me is for another book) and so Mr. Light could be reasonably assured that there would be paragraphs with words spelled correctly in sentences that ended in a period and had a subject, predicate and verb.

We wrote these columns together. We do not write every other word together, but we edit each other—with a light touch—and it will probably be easy for you to determine who wrote which. Barbara and I are a team.

Our marriage survived, and our lives have thrived. San Diego is a wonderful place to be an entrepreneur. Our community understands that a failed company is part of an entrepreneur's journey. After the news company went out of business, we would go to community events, and people would say to us, "We know that you tried hard. What are you doing next?"

Now Barbara is about to launch a new career in the political arena. I am working harder than ever as a venture capitalist focused on seed financings. I have a job again, and I love what I do.

Most importantly, a big part of our lives is focused on the next generation of entrepreneurs. We have taught entrepreneurship at UC San Diego, we mentor students and entrepreneurs of all ages, and I've spoken at The Miramar Brig several times (these experiences are recounted in three columns in the book).

This book includes some of our favorite columns.

After you read the book, we'd love to hear from you about your experiences, insights and challenges.

Sincerely,
Neil
neil@blackbirdv.com

A NOTE FROM BARBARA:

As I look back at my life, I believe that a large part of my business success is due to the fact that I ended up in San Diego in a community that is welcoming to newcomers if they have passion, energy and are willing to work hard. During my years with CONNECT, I had the opportunity to work with and learn from our region's leading entrepreneurs.

When Neil and I started our first software company, we were able to tap into the expertise of the collaborative ecosystem that had evolved, in large part because of CONNECT. At the beginning of ProFlowers, when I was the vice president of marketing for one of the early e-commerce start-ups, I found other San Diegans willing to share their expertise.

My entrepreneurial spirit stems from my mother Adelaide Bry who was a woman ahead of her time. During World War II, she was Rosie the Riveter, an editor at an aviation magazine, and a radio talk show host. After she got divorced in the 1960s, she went to work full-time, and she became the first woman vice president at a large Philadelphia ad agency. Initially, she was paid less than comparable men, and there was nothing she could do about it. She wanted to buy a house that she could easily afford, and she still had to get a male friend to co-sign on the mortgage. Sadly she died of pancreatic cancer in 1983 when my oldest daughter, her first grandchild, was two years old.

From my mother, I learned that a woman could succeed in the business world, and I also learned about the importance of re-invention. The same year that I graduated from college, she was awarded a Master's degree in psychology, and she went on to have another successful career as an author, therapist and consultant.

I'm blessed to have had many chapters in my life—high school teacher, journalist, entrepreneurship center executive, entrepreneur, angel investor, community volunteer, mother, wife, and now grandmother! It's wonderful to have participated in the San Diego innovation economy for almost 30 years, and I'm looking forward to my next chapter in the political world.

Sincerely,
Barbara
bbry@blackbirdv.com

ENTREPRENEURS HAVE NO CHOICE—IT'S IN THEIR DNA
September 13, 2011

You all know what DNA is—the genetic code of life, the Watson/Crick double helix that you learned about in high school. If you can't blame your life on your parents, then for sure, you can blame it on your Deoxyribonucleic acid.

Now, an NDA is quite another matter. That stands for non-disclosure agreement, and it is what entrepreneurs often ask you to sign before they will show you their idea for the next big thing.

A recent *The Wall Street Journal* article decried the loss of the entrepreneur class.

According to data cited in the article, the total number of "births" of new businesses declined sharply this year from previous years, and more people who were self-employed failed and left self-employment than people who entered.

But a proper distinction was made by Steven Kaplan, who teaches entrepreneurship at the Booth Business School at the University of Chicago. He pointed out there is "a real dichotomy between the technology economy versus the meat and potato economy."

You betcha. We would like to suggest that this thing called entrepreneurship cannot be taught and that using that word or that character trait in the same manner as the pundits talk about "small business in America" is completely false. Entrepreneurship is clearly different from starting a small business like a restaurant. In our minds, an entrepreneur sees opportunity where others don't and/or comes up with a new approach to solving a problem.

As for teaching entrepreneurship, we try to do just that at the von Liebig Center for Entrepreneurism and Technology Advancement at UC San Diego's Jacobs School of Engineering, and what we say in the first sentence of the first class is that we cannot teach you to be an entrepreneur. What we can do is teach the principles of entrepreneurship. We can help someone to think in an entrepreneurial way. But the thing itself, we do not believe can be taught.

It is in one's DNA. It is the way you are wired. It is imprinted early on, if not at birth, then shortly thereafter.

Now, this theory may be a bit out there for some folks, so we went and tested it with Dr. Soren Solari, Ph.D., integrative neuroscience from UC San Diego.

Saying that being an entrepreneur is "in the blood" of your DNA is surely a scientific fact, contends Solari, who adds, "The harder question is where is its origin."

He suggests that this "need to achieve" is actually wired into the nervous system. In particular, he gives credence to the power of experiences from birthright up to this moment in one's life. "Epigenetics says that your DNA is not only made up of the DNA of your grandparents and most distant ancestors, but also of the experiences of your parents, so you have this blend of genetics and experience."

This is heady stuff indeed, and what we can tell you is that this entrepreneur thing is not really a conscious decision. It is who you are. Entrepreneurship demands to be embraced when it forces itself upon you just the way a great musician is forced to play music. If you saw Hershey Felder play Leonard Bernstein in the recent production of "Maestro" at the Old Globe, you know what we mean. Bernstein had no choice. He was compelled to pursue a career in music.

LA JOLLA BOOKSTORE HOLDS ITS OWN AGAINST GIANTS BY RE-INVENTING

September 22, 2014

The bookstore is dead. Long live the bookstore.

One La Jolla bookstore has triumphed in the face of the big chain stores, in the face of Amazon, and in the face of e-books. Meet Nancy Warwick, owner of Warwick's, which is believed to be the oldest continuously family-owned and operated bookstore in the United States. When she was growing up, Nancy, now 51, remembers seven bookstores operating in the village of La Jolla. Today, there are only two—Warwick's and D.G. Wills—that specialize in new and used scholarly books.

The history of Warwick's is fascinating. The original store—called Redding's—was established in 1902 by Warwick's great grandmother Genevieve Redding and her husband. Nancy's great grandfather William T. (known as W.T.) owned a bookstore in Waterloo, Iowa. When he moved to La Jolla in 1939, he purchased Redding's, married Genevieve and renamed the store Warwick's. Three generations later, Nancy Warwick took over from her parents. It seems she was destined to go into the "family business."

We talked with Nancy and two of her key team members—Adrian Newell, a book buyer, and Julie Slavinsky, director of events and community relations—in the small second floor office in which Nancy and her sister Cathy (a schoolteacher who owns 10 percent of the business) first made bows and boxes for gifts when they were growing up. What is clear is that Nancy and her team are passionate about books.

"We helped with inventory, we rode the dumb waiter between the first and second floor, and we went to gift shows. We were involved but not pressured. I never expected to own and run the store. My parents said you have to love the store to run it," said Warwick.

Warwick left San Diego to attend UC Santa Barbara and then earned a Ph.D. in anthropology from UCLA. She was living in Los Angeles with her husband and son Zachary in 1997 when her parents told her that they planned to retire. For a year and a half, she commuted between Los Angeles and San Diego and finally moved back to San Diego with her family in 1998, at a precipitous time in the book business. **Amazon.com** had started in 1994 and was beginning to gain traction.

"In the 1990s, we were hurt by the big chain stores like Barnes and Noble and Crown. Then in the fall of 1998, e-readers became more easy to use," Warwick said. The 2008 recession also took a toll so the store has continually had to reinvent itself, she said.

Warwick's has survived by offering a wide range of products (books, gifts and office supplies), providing personal service, paying careful attention to inventory, and increasing the number of author events. In addition, Nancy said, "La Jolla is a fabulous location, and we have an educated and loyal customer group."

Famous authors hosted by Warwick's include former Secretary of State Hillary Clinton, actor Kirk Douglas, U.S. Supreme Court Justice Sonia Sotomayor, and entertainer Ozzy Osbourne. The store has developed community partnerships to market the events and sometimes holds them off-site in large venues.

"Our goal is to have a healthy vibrant business with a lot of customer support even if it means that we grow less. We want to stay true to our identity, and our book department is key. However, we've changed what we emphasize. For example, travel books used to be important but now that's an area that's easy to research online. We used to sell a lot of photo albums and invitations, but those have moved online," Warwick said. The store now offers more children's books and nonfiction books that are visually appealing. Warwick's has 39 employees.

Warwick and her team say it's hard to compete against **Amazon. com**, a company that is valued at over $150 billion and yet is barely profitable, so they focus on providing excellent personal service. "I have customers who come looking for me and ask for my recommendations. The personal connection is everything. That's an experience you won't get from an algorithm," Slavinsky said.

Rule #371:
You cannot outsource
the human touch.

CASTING FOR SUCCESS, LIKE CASTING FOR STEELHEAD, IS ART

April 25, 2012

Oncorhynchus mykiss. Or more commonly known as the rainbow trout. Its close cousin, the steelhead, is a sea-run rainbow trout (anadromous) that returns to the fresh water river, where it was first born, to spawn after two to three years at sea.

I recently spent three days on the Nehalem River outside Tillamook, Oregon, chasing the steelhead, and the experience provided some echoes to the entrepreneurial challenge we all face.

First, there is a reason they call it fishing, instead of catching. Fly-fishing for steelhead is not about catching; it is about the art and beauty of the cast. The catching part is to a large extent luck.

We used a spey rod. It was 13 feet long, and the cast was supposed to launch the fly about 90 feet across the river. It is a two-handed cast, with its own ballet twist and turn ritual. There is a delicate rhythm; apply too much power too quickly and the fly falls in a ball tangled in front of you or hooks you in the ear.

Well, creating a product is like that cast. It is an art; it has its own elegance. Find the graceful transfer of effort to create power in your company. Form follows function. Delight in the presentation, in the sheer joy of being able to cast the fly a very long way with a beautiful, final finish. There is serenity and gratification in creating a great product—just like a great cast. When it all works and the fly lands far out on the river, there is a yelp of joy—unbridled enthusiasm simply in the doing, in the being able to make something that meets the test, in making something that someone wants to use or touch or buy.

Raising money, on the other hand, is like catching. Presentation of the fly matters greatly. However, casting where there are no fish is an exercise in futility, except, you can't know if there are no fish. You have to assume that every cast is right on the nose, with a pink flashabou pattern that they cannot resist. But then there is no take. Like pitching your PowerPoint to the angels who don't fund or the venture capitalists who say they have money, but really don't. They just like to look at the fly. That way they can collect their fees.

So you have to love the pitch, you have to love the process, you have to love your team, your company and your product, because even making 700 casts (as I did on the trip)—many of them beautiful—does not guarantee a bite.

Finally, one member of our group caught a very nice steelhead from a terrible, tangled cast. Luck and timing. It doesn't seem fair. And isn't that the whole story of the startup. You fail many more times than you succeed, and the favorable outcome is often a fortuitous pivot from a failed idea. It can make you crazy. Why isn't there a clear, connected, linear correlation between effort, conception, execution, production, acceptance and catching? There isn't, and after all these years at the game, I have finally come to believe that is just the way it ought to be.

It's not a puzzle you can solve. That's why you keep coming back. Just like the steelhead that keeps coming back up the river, against the current, so he can spawn and go back into the ocean, and then a few years later, come back up the river to spawn again—and again.

Be the fish.

That's fly-fishing for entrepreneurs.

Rule #208:
Never, ever underestimate
the power of good fortune.

Rule #213:
Never, ever underestimate
the power of time and timing.

HARD WORK, PATIENCE, CAN PAY OFF

January 12, 2015

Friends, family and fools are usually the first money for your business. Let's assume you do not have any of those. The next best thing is to grow your business organically. That is a $5 concept that means reinvesting the net cash flow from one month into the next one, often building your business more slowly—and keeping the ownership primarily under your own control.

Meet structural engineer Simon Wong, who started Simon Wong Engineering on Dec. 3, 1986, in a 120-square-foot windowless office in a Mission Valley executive suite. He was 28 years old and had only a few years of work experience. As he recalls, "I was young. I thought that if I don't make it, I could always find another job." (Neil's note: The time to take the risk is when you can most afford it.)

Flash forward to 2015, and you find that Simon Wong Engineering has participated in many of our region's biggest construction projects and has 120 employees. Projects include the new construction at San Diego's Lindbergh Field, the Carlsbad desalination plant, the San Diego Metro Biosolids Center, and the Oceanside to Escondido Sprinter rail project. The company's three divisions are structural engineering, bridge engineering and construction management.

To ensure the continued success of the company, Wong decided to merge in 2012 with Kleinfelder Inc., an employee-owned, multi-discipline engineering firm with offices all over the United States and the world. Wong believed that the cultures of the two organizations would blend well and that the combination would fuel continued growth. After the merger, Kleinfelder moved its corporate headquarters to San Diego, and Wong currently serves as vice president of the company. (Neil's note: A great way to scale is to find the right strategic partner. It is not always raising more money.)

When he was 17 years old, Wong emigrated from Hong Kong to Reno, Nev., where he finished high school. Next he majored in engineering at the University of Nevada-Reno, where he also earned a master's degree.

He decided to move to San Diego in 1985, and a year later, started his own company. To drum up business, he "cold called" potential customers. No job was too small, and every customer's satisfaction was important. Through referrals from happy customers and more outreach, his business grew and by the end of the first year, he employed a drafter and a junior engineer.

Wong was always active in the community, and in 1992 he was a co-founder of the Asian Business Association of San Diego. "For a long time the Asian community in San Diego was divided into Chinese, Japanese, Korean and Vietnamese groups. A few of us thought that having a group that represented the business interests of all Asians was a good idea. There were similar organizations in Los Angeles and San Francisco," he said. "Giving back to the community is vital for every business person since the community gives you the opportunity."

Through the ABA, he made connections that helped his business. But what's important is that his focus was always on helping others.

Over the years, he brought in five partners who owned a share of the business because Wong believed that it would make the company more successful. Being willing to share the pie is one of our most important rules.

Another part of his philosophy—his willingness to work as a subcontractor on large government contracts—has also been important. "It's how we got our first government business. Part of a job is better than no job at all. As you start accumulating experience and learning more about a particular agency, you can become a prime contractor," he said.

Wong understood that different customers have different priorities. Some customers focus on price. Others need a job completed by a specific date. He believes that a large part of his success is having the flexibility to adjust. Listening to the customer and then understanding what they really want is key.

Wong's story is classic—an immigrant, smart, hard work, a couple of lucky breaks, community, coupled with being both patient and passionate. That is a tough combination to beat.

Rule #385:
Play for the long game.

PITCH AS SWIFT AS AN ELEVATOR RIDE CRUCIAL TO GETTING OFF THE GROUND

January 15, 2013

Every entrepreneur is coached to have an elevator pitch—a compelling, captivating, and concise story about you or your company that you can tell in the time it takes to go up or down in an elevator—30 seconds for a suburban office building, 60 seconds for a downtown high-rise, and two to three minutes for an elevator with a lot of stops. If you happen to be in the elevator with Mark Cuban or Dave McClure and they ask what you do, you need to have an answer that hooks them.

"Her husband had beaten her so badly that she feared for her life. To escape her desperate situation, Lana got on a Greyhound bus in Florida, with $17 and her 4-year-old daughter and came to San Diego where she didn't know a soul. What led up to that moment? Years of abuse and thoughts of: I'm not good enough, I'm not smart enough. I can't make it on my own."

How does that grab you? That is the opening by Dana Bristol-Smith, founder and executive director of Leap to Success, who was the first-place winner at the recent fast-pitch competition for nonprofits sponsored by San Diego Social Venture Partners.

Recognizing the importance of elevator pitches for the non-profit community, SDSVP provided 20 semifinalists out of 85 applicants with intensive coaching and mentoring to help them convey their impact in three minutes. Ten finalists then competed at a live event for $40,000 in cash prizes plus $10,000 of in-kind services. Leap to Success was awarded $25,000 for first place.

In the process, the winner, Bristol-Smith, learned, "Your story is a flower that is just getting ready to bloom. There has to be a buildup. You have to convey that your organization is on the verge of something big. You want people to feel it emotionally so that they will take action and want to take part in what you're doing."

Here are some thoughts on the infamous elevator.

No buzz words, no fluff, and no arrogance, as in "We are the leading provider of _____." That is not true. If you were the leading provider, you would not be pitching for pennies in an elevator.

Tell me what problem you are solving. "We make _____ and it addresses the problem of _____."

Who is the customer, and what suggests that said customer will pay anything for your "change the world" solution?

After punching the audience in the gut with her opening, Bristol-Smith explained that Leap to Success provides training, life coaching, and mentoring for abused women by teaching them "four powerful tools—goal setting and action planning toward jobs or education; reframing negative thoughts to go from "I can't" to "I can"; assertive communication to stand up for themselves and their children; and public speaking skills to build confidence and share their own stories and empower others."

Lastly, do not get off the elevator without the Ask. Be concrete and specific.

Bristol-Smith said, "We are looking for investors to raise $1 million. Ten thousand dollars will change the futures of 10 women and their families, five angels at $100,000 each will fund expansion to reach more than 10,000 families."

A customer testimonial can also be helpful, and in Bristol-Smith's case, she offered the audience a surprise, as the real Lana joined her on stage, and she said, "Today I'm a different person. I am no longer a victim . . . I have the privilege of mentoring women who are just like me."

Expert assistance and an outsider's perspective can be helpful in drafting your elevator pitch. "I give a lot of presentations in the community, and this process helped me," said Trisha Gooch, director of development and community relations for Second Chance, which provides job readiness and life-skills training and won the second prize of $10,000.

"I learned how to better engage the audience when you're on stage and you don't have a podium, and how to memorize a presentation and still seem natural," said Elizabeth Schott, executive director of micro-lender Accion San Diego, which won the third prize of $5,000.

Rule #151:

Plan for a quick ride,
but if the elevator should happen to get stuck between floors,
have a pen and a term sheet ready.

PITCHING IDEA HARD ENOUGH; TRY DOING IT IN SIGN LANGUAGE

May 20, 2013

Most of us take hearing and speaking for granted. Don't.

It is hard enough to pitch your idea with words. Now imagine doing it in sign language.

Speaking in sign language with an interpreter, graduate student Isidore Niyongabo won $15,000 (the highest amount awarded) in the recent University of San Diego Social Innovation Challenge (SIC) for his International Deaf Education Advocacy and Leadership (IDEAL) program that addresses the issue of educating the estimated 57 million deaf people in developing countries, most of whom currently have no access to education. He also won an additional $2,500 for getting the most texted votes in Qualcomm Labs' Audience Choice Contest.

Niyongabo's personal story is inspirational. He grew up in Burundi in East Africa and lost his hearing at the age of 10 after suffering from spinal meningitis. Through the efforts of his father, who later, sadly, became a genocide victim, he received an education in Burundi and then came to the United States, where he graduated from San Diego State University in 2010.

Interest in starting social enterprises is growing, and the University of San Diego has taken a leadership role in fostering their development both through its academic programs and the establishment of an annual Social Innovation Challenge, now in its third year.

Social enterprises are organizations (both for-profit and non-profit) whose primary purpose is the common good, according to the Social Enterprise Alliance. These organizations use the methods and disciplines of business—including the establishment of measurable goals—and the power of the marketplace to advance their social, environmental and human justice agendas.

The prize money allows Niyongabo to develop an online resource in conjunction with the first East Africa Deaf Youth Leadership Summit that will take place in June in Uganda. He has already raised the funding for the conference, and the 50 participants between the ages of 18 and 30 have been selected by their communities in Burundi, Rwanda, Tanzania, Kenya and Uganda. At the summit, they will be trained on how to become advocates, leaders and mentors so that they can return home and guide others.

The long-term goals of IDEAL are to increase the number of deaf students accepted into universities, receiving educational scholarships, and getting jobs. Niyongabo's team and advisers includes both people who can hear and deaf people.

As we've written before, your own experience is sometimes the genesis for starting a business. This is true in the case of Connor Lind, a junior majoring in mechanical engineering, who was awarded $8,500 for Roam—which he describes as "Yelp" for volunteering.

While in high school, Lind started doing international volunteer work when he had the opportunity to go on a Habitat for Humanity trip to Poland. Another volunteer opportunity came out of a chance meeting with a USD professor who connected him to a Buddhist nunnery in the Himalayas, where he taught English last summer.

"Roam came out of my desire to share these opportunities and to make them more accessible for other people by having volunteers share their personal experiences," said Lind. "There are vast databases of nonprofits but no way to figure out how to assess the quality of a volunteer experience and which ones are legitimate and which ones aren't."

Graduate student Teresa Smith, the SIC winner in 2012, won this year's $10,000 Verizon Green Award for the Safe Parking program that provides a safe designated place with support services for transitional homeless living in their vehicles.

Last year, she won for her mobile food truck business that provides healthy food to homeless individuals. The "Fresh" truck currently operates at lunchtime during the week and makes three stops—at the Neil Good Day Center, Winter Shelter Tent and 14th Street and Imperial Avenue. This summer, Smith plans to expand into dinner service and potentially Saturdays. About half of the customers pay with food stamps and the other half with cash.

Rule #52:
If you can do well at the same time you do good— that is the next big thing.

ENTREPRENEURS CAN LEARN A LOT FROM MAGICIANS
August 4, 2014

"Follow the money"—the most famous words delivered by Deep Throat during Watergate.

I recently funded a biotech startup started by a UC San Diego genius who has developed a novel and inexpensive way to determine whether a drug is the real deal—in other words, whether it is counterfeit or genuine.

This appears to be innovative technology and solves a real problem, but in classic startup fashion, we could not solve the core business problem of "who cares" and its corollary, "who is going to pay for this?" After our first foray into due diligence, we learned that in North America, consumers, hospitals, and doctors weren't interested.

Allow me now to digress and discuss magic and magicians, and I am going to draw on some research from Harvard Business School professor Stefan Thomke, who teaches innovation in partnership with Jason Randal, a famous magician/mentalist.

Magicians are constantly under pressure to reinvent themselves. If David Copperfield makes the Statue of Liberty disappear, then Franz Haray tops it by making the space shuttle vanish. The same is true of leaders in innovative companies. Everyone is looking for the "wow" factor. And Thomke argues that innovative companies can benefit from what magicians do.

Magicians spend a lot of time considering which illusion will bring the most bang for the buck. The corollary for startups is to discover the "real problem that you are solving for." Walt Disney famously did not worry first about rides, parking, or food. Walt worried only about giving his "customers a magical experience."

Thomke continues, "The solution to a problem often comes from the most unlikely sources." This, of course, argues for Rule #3 of our book that says, "You need to go to all the meetings and events, in particular the ones you are sure will be a total waste of time." It is the intersection of low expectations and random chance when solutions or innovation most often appears.

The magician often uses distraction or misdirection in order to entertain and delight. You never see anyone at Disney World take out the trash. They do it through an underground series of tunnels.

Randal, the magician, says, "Sell the experience." The masters in this area of "patter" are Penn and Teller. Their talking is as important as the illusion. And only Penn talks. Teller never says a word.

The innovation is not only the technology or the science. It is the ability to tap into people's emotions and make the consumer feel good about the product. Think about packaging and then look at high-end vodka bottles. The stuff inside is still only vodka but the bottles are art.

And Thomke and Randal bring us to storytelling. There are hundreds of "pitch fests" in this town, and the key skill is how to tell the story. The great magicians embed the trick into the storytelling.

My partner and I see lots of deals, and often the innovation is intriguing, but the storyteller isn't very good. So my suggestion to young entrepreneurs is to work on learning to "sell the sizzle, not the steak." Practice in front of a mirror. Harry Houdini owned hundreds of locks, and he rehearsed picking them in front of a mirror—a reversed image to improve his skills.

How can I make it better? Thomke argues that MP3 was great technology, but it was Apple that took it to the next level and developed iTunes. Persistence and continuing to ask how can I dazzle the customer proved to be the winning hand.

Now let's return to my new biotech. The solution to the problem appeared in a strange way. I went fishing with my son-in-law. On the boat was a man who turned out—just by chance—to know something about biotech and China. After two meetings, we engaged him to join the team.

It turned out that we had been looking in the wrong direction. The magic solution was not in North America, but in the rest of the world where counterfeiting is a problem. We followed the money, and it led to the insurance companies that pay the bill for a real drug when a counterfeit is used. We had the classic problem—interesting technology looking for a business model. We found it on a boat in the ocean along with eight lovely yellowtail.

Rule #365:
Magicians will not tell you how they do the trick, but seeing is still believing.

A DAY IN SILICON VALLEY

March 16, 2015

"Good morning, I'm Dave Wandishin, and I'll be your captain on this flight today."

Now we all know about customer service, but that speech was delivered in the terminal, at the gate, before boarding the plane.

We were flying on Virgin America to San Francisco for a touch of *Ferris Bueller's Day Off* and to chase the elusive venture capitalist for a half-baked scheme that I am backing—and out comes this handsome fellow who went around and offered to comfort young fliers or anybody who had a question. Before we got on the plane.

Not a muzzled, muffled disconnected voice over the intercom from the cockpit. No other airline does this. And I can tell you that he absolutely charmed the crowd. There is a lesson here—but don't tell Delta or United. Great customer service starts early in the sales cycle.

So we had our day in the valley and it reminded us of what F. Scott Fitzgerald said to Hemingway, "The rich are different than you and me." And Ernie retorted, "Yes, they have more money."

In truth, we were reasonably successful in our begging, and we did get our hands on some of their dough. But there is a cautionary note, and it comes from Rich Karlgaard, who writes for Forbes. He calls the piece "Late Bloomers in Peril," and the theme is that Silicon Valley has dangerously tilted to the temple of ultimate STEM and its young acolytes.

He channels the Super Bowl and reminds us that neither Russell Wilson nor Tom Brady were highly rated in high school. Brady was a sixth-round pick in the NFL. He mentions Raymond Chandler, who was 51 when he wrote his first novel, "The Big Sleep."

He asks if the young tech billionaires really inspire and capture our imagination or do they intimidate. Note that Bill Hewlett barely got into college, Steve Jobs and Bill Gates dropped out of college and Andy Grove went to City College of New York.

Karlgaard ends with his opinion that Silicon Valley has morphed into Algorithmic Valley. Maybe—and that brings us to the end of our day.

After our "pitch" sessions, we were invited (I am sure by mistake) to a fancy party given by Formation 8, a very hot venture fund (Joe Lonsdale, Palantir), held at the St. Regis. We hid our AARP cards in our pockets to make sure that we could get in. But whoa, Fitzgerald was right.

It was hip and loud and filled with beautiful people who were doing "startups." We talked to Caroline Ghosen, whose company, Levo League, is trying to help young people in the early stages of their career with mentorship. Sort of LinkedIn for millennials. She said she had raised a seed round of $9 million from angels. We don't have those kinds of wings in San Diego.

And then I got the ultimate put-down. I asked a young man for a business card, and I was told, "I don't carry one; we don't use paper." If I had used the word Rolodex, I would have been asked to leave the room.

There is a dichotomy in the valley. Our country knows that it must promote STEM in our schools, but by the same token, if you were not of the very elite, the Harvard/Stanford/MIT, then you may feel somewhat marginalized, which explains in part why STEM education in America trails other countries. Our idols are still athletes and actors, not Henry Ford and Thomas Edison.

And it is a recognized truth that many of the most successful companies today were started by second and third attempts from the fabled entrepreneurs. No one bats 1.000.

My dad always said I was a late bloomer. I took that to mean that he did not really think I would ever amount to anything. It was a nice way of diminishing both his expectations and mine.

Well, what I can tell you is that baseball is a nine-inning game, and you get a certain number of at bats—regardless of the early score.

Finally, we flew back on Virgin, and when we landed, my bride, Ms. Bry, and I let out a collective sigh and spoke the line from the "Wizard of Oz": "There's no place like home. There's no place like home. There's no place like home."

Rule #394:
Maybe we are not in Silicon Valley,
but we are not in Kansas, either.

THE RIGHT SCIENCE, PERSISTENCE, CLEAR VISION CAN BRING IN BIG BUCKS

July 8, 2013

I'll see your $40 million and raise you $5 million.

Even though total venture capital funding is down, a few startup biotechnology companies are raising staggering amounts of early money from traditional venture firms and corporate pharmaceutical funds. What sets these companies apart is their focus on science that has groundbreaking potential and the extensive experience of both their management and scientific teams.

In May, San Diego-based Effector Therapeutics announced $45 million in a Series A financing on the first day that it opened the doors, and its story contains many valuable lessons for entrepreneurs.

The story begins with the sale of Anadys Pharmaceuticals to pharmaceutical giant Roche in December 2011, and the desire of now-former Anadys CEO Steve Worland to do another startup. We understand this urge since Neil suffers from a similar affliction. You want the next company to solve bigger problems, and you want to avoid the mistakes that you made in the earlier one.

In an organized way, Worland set out to learn about the most exciting science being conducted at top research institutes, and simultaneously he met with 50 venture capitalists to learn what they were paying attention to. Most of the VCs said they preferred to fund individual products and not make a large investment to build an infrastructure company, yet Worland's dream was to start a company with potentially transformative (and not yet proven) technology. We admire Worland's methodical approach and his aspiration to solve a big problem.

Note: He talked to the money while he went looking for the science.

Within a few months, Worland focused on a group of UC San Francisco scientists who were working on the cell's effector mechanism. Worland believed that their research could lead to the development of a new class of small molecule drugs that could selectively regulate protein synthesis, also known as translation, and could be used to treat cancer. He particularly liked that UCSF researcher Kevan Shokat was also the co-founder of two biotechnology companies—Cellular Genomics (sold to Gilead Sciences) and Intellikine (sold to Takeda Pharmaceuticals)—an indication of an entrepreneurial spirit and an understanding of industry's needs.

"Shokat talked about inventing drugs in a way that is uncommon in academics, a way that usually requires 10 to 20 years of industry experience," said Worland. Worland also got to know Shokat's colleague Davide Ruggero, and through a series of discussions, the idea for the company evolved. We have also found that most good ideas are the product of several conversations—not a one-time flash insight.

Once Worland believed the technology could be the genesis of a company, he discussed the licensing issues with the UCSF Technology Transfer Office (the agreement was finished in a few weeks), and in parallel, he talked to potential investors.

Note: To all tech transfer offices—see above. "Done in a few weeks."

"You keep refining the story as you meet new people. It's an evolutionary process," said Worland, who estimated that he made 50 investor pitches. "I had to learn how to explain the story to excite the venture capitalists. Later people said to me, 'Why didn't you explain it to me that way the first time around?'"

Note: 50 pitches is normal. The more you pitch, the better and tighter and cleaner the story becomes. The feedback and questions you get are essential in making your plan better.

Rule #251:
Pitch to the least desired investors first. Practice in Boston before opening on Broadway.

Seventeen months after selling Anadys and 14 months after meeting Shokat and Ruggero, Effector Therapeutics closed a $45 million financing round from U.S. Venture Partners, Abingworth, Novartis Venture Funds, SR One, Astellas Venture Management, Osage University Partners and Mission Bay Capital. None are based in San Diego.

The funding is enough money to last four to five years through the first clinical study—a significant milestone.

Worland chose to locate Effector in San Diego because the region "has a lot of talent (and a dearth of local capital) so if you can bring money, you get the pick of the crop in contrast with the Bay Area and Boston where it's more competitive." Now his focus is on hiring the right people and creating an egalitarian culture in which "we're going to rip apart every experiment and no one can have an ego," in contrast to the hierarchical nature of academia.

Rule #254:
Big (talented) team, big idea, big money and small egos.
A vision for success.

HARD WORK, EAR TOWARD CUSTOMERS, HAVE BAKERY OWNERS BRINGING IN DOUGH

February 23, 2015

"Man shall not live on bread alone."—Matthew 4:4

On the other hand, a really good challah is worth looking for, and when I moved to Carmel Valley in 1995, one of the first places that I shopped was the new Village Mill Bakery. It made some of the best challah I've ever eaten, and even though I don't live in Carmel Valley anymore, I'm still a regular customer.

Defying the odds and statistics that are more tilted toward failure, they have survived in a family business for over 20 years, so I decided to talk with the owners—the founder Sandra Pike and her husband, Parker,—about their experiences and how they managed to thrive.

In 1994, Sandra moved to San Diego from Wisconsin to join one of the early online mortgage companies. After the company failed, Sandra wanted to stay here, so she decided to open a bakery even though her only experience was in her own kitchen. "It was one of those decisions that was so clear even though it made no sense," she recalled. At the time, she was dating Parker, whom she had met on a blind date. They got married in 1998.

(Neil's note: Clearly, this supports the theory that the way to a man's heart is through his stomach.)

To learn about the bakery business, she visited a lot of them ("I saw the tired faces, but I didn't think that it would last forever"), considered joining a franchise and decided that the business wouldn't support paying a 7 percent franchise fee. A rigorous student of business (look before you leap), Sandra also attended a month-long cooking school in Paris where she learned about making products that contained a lot of butter. Ultimately, she decided that Village Mill should make healthier products, and she worked with a business consultant who helped her with the original formulas and the equipment purchases. (Neil's note: She was ahead of her time. Healthy vs. butter—no contest.)

The initial capital was $90,000—the entire amount of her IRA—and a $160,000 Small Business Administration loan that was guaranteed by the equity she had in two condominiums. She was all in. For the first few years, this was her life seven days a week:

- Come in at 1 a.m. to start baking and work until 8 a.m.

- Go to Parker's condo three blocks away and sleep when he was at work.

- Return to Village Mill in the early afternoon, work until closing time at 6 p.m. and then finish paperwork.

- Return to Parker's condominium and sleep until 1 a.m.

"I realized that it's hard to have a personal life. I used to go shopping and go to the movies. I didn't do those things anymore," she said.

Sleep deprivation was a price that she paid in order to grow the business. Parker proposed to her at a Padres game on the Jumbotron during the sixth inning. Sandra was so tired that she had fallen asleep in the second inning and wanted to leave, and Parker had to convince her to stay. After being hospitalized twice for exhaustion, she decided to close Village Mill on Sundays.

Today, she works more-reasonable hours, although the couple has not taken a full week of vacation in 20 years. As the business has grown, Village Mill has been able to hire good staff including customer service manager JoAnn Wornham and lead baker Antonio Godines, who have been there 16 years.

Listening to your customer is one of our favorite mantras, and Sandra has always done that.

When a local rabbi suggested that she make challah, she said, "What is challah?" She quickly learned and now makes several flavors including chocolate, which was suggested by another rabbi's wife. All together, challah is the best-selling product. She launched a wholesale operation that Parker runs in his off hours from his regular job teaching marketing at UC San Diego Extension.

In addition to working long hours and selling a quality product, she attributes part of her success to effectively using QuickBooks and Excel to monitor the business operations. "You have to have your hand on the money, the people and the technology on a daily basis," she said.

Village Mill recently moved into a new location on the upper level of the Del Mar Highlands Town Center. On her first day in September 1995, she said the business took in $220—and it earned about $125,000 in revenue for the first year. Currently, annual revenues are about $800,000.

In talking with the Pikes, it is evident that they are devoted both to each other and to Village Mill. They clearly know which side their bread is buttered on.

Rule #389:
If you want to be the chef of your own life,
spend time in the kitchen.

TV'S SHARK TANK IS THEATER, YET INSTRUCTIVE

February 16, 2015

Rule #388:

You can never have too many dots.

I have been watching the television show *Shark Tank*, and I love it.

I am fascinated by the range of deals—inflatable balls, food trucks, sauces, cosmetics—and a guy even shows up with a hollow golf club that you can urinate into when you are on the course. Only in America.

But what fascinates me the most is not the sharks. Rather it is the supplicants and how they make decisions—how they value their companies, deciding when to say yes to the sharks and how to negotiate. My charming and brilliant wife was actually yelling at the television a few weeks ago, telling the person "to take the deal, are you crazy, say yes now."

Of course, the show is theater and it is manipulative, but it is also instructive. Mr. Wonderful, Kevin O'Leary, is the tough guy. He asks hard questions about revenue, product, margin, valuation, etc. I love this guy. If you come in with a crazy pre-money valuation, his only comment is "you are dead to me."

The shark on the far right, Robert Herjavec, is always polite, but is also quick to drop a deal if the entrepreneur hesitates. The two women, Barbara Corcoran, real estate magnate, is tough, and her counterpart, Lori Greiner, of QVC fame, is a bit more cerebral. And there is Mark Cuban, who makes decisions in seconds. Daymond John, of FUBU fame, is contemplative. I recommend that entrepreneurs watch the show.

Here are some recent "minnow" stories from the trenches of yours truly.

Two young women pitched my partner and me on the phone last week. The pitch was terrible. My partner and I were charming (in our opinion), but ruthless. They did not answer the questions, they did not know their numbers, and they were not prepared. But after the call was done, I called back 10 minutes later and told them why we passed—and then remembering the sharks, I offered to let them come back in person and try again. Somehow, I think there might be a pony in there.

I have another company that needed a chief executive officer. We were desperate to the point that if we couldn't find the right guy, we were going to bag the company. And then we caught a break. Right out of Central Casting, a guy with a perfect résumé to match shows up—a referral from a friend—on the second try. When this happens, don't change your underwear. Breathe through your eyelids, buy a lottery ticket, and go to Vegas. It is a "rara avis" indeed.

Dear entrepreneur, the problem is never the deal or the product or the market: it is the team. I know there is a demand for software developers, but being a founder is not the same as being the CEO. The gating factor to funding is having the right person in the right seat on the right bus going in the right direction. Finding the bus, buying the bus, or painting the bus is not the same as steering the bus.

Recently, I founded a company that was cute, goofy, well-intentioned, and a complete and utter failure. In December, I was reading a *New York Times* story about charity and one of the genius gurus in the story was a professor at University of California San Diego. I chased him down, hired him, and rebuilt the company around him.

The second incarnation is funded and has a real chance to be gigantic. All that was required was a simple pivot. However, the theme here is that entrepreneurs need to read and study lots of sources, not just TechCrunch or Reddit. Information is never neatly packaged and what appear to be the random connections that are so powerful are never really random.

They result from connecting the dots—and you need to collect disparate dots from lots of places before you can connect them.

The above stories seem like I was just incredibly lucky. I was. But I am a voracious and relentless dot collector.

SAN DIEGO BIKE REPAIR ENTREPRENEUR IS WEAVING HIS WAY TO SUCCESS

July 28, 2014

The wheel is always spinning—especially if you are a bicycle. San Diego is a bike friendly town. We have bike lanes, triathlons, a velodrome, and multiple groups that ride—the Wheelmen, the Cyclo-Vets, the Swami Riders, bike clubs from UCSD and SDSU, and many more. We have events—the Cruiser Ride, the Ramona Fun Ride, and the North County Roadies. San Diego is awash in bicycles and spandex. And all bikes need repair and maintenance.

Meet Anywhere Bicycle Repair and Stu Clott, the owner. My interest in Mr. Clott started a few years ago when I wanted someone to come to my office and tune up my bike. Like a doctor in days of yore, Clott makes house calls. He backs up the word "anywhere."

And here is his story of how he turned his passion into a viable business.

Clott's experience fixing bikes started during high school outside of Philadelphia. He dropped out of college after one year and then attended one year of a technical vocation school. In 2004, he drove his Nissan Frontier mini-truck across the country to San Diego so he could live in a place where he could ride his bike year round.

Clott quickly landed a job in a local bike shop, and over the next six years, he worked in five different places. "In every shop I was dumbfounded at how slow their service department was because of their systems, not because of their workers. Their focus was selling bikes, not repairing them. I thought that San Diegans had a right to expect both high quality repair, as well as fast turn-around," he said.

As Clott moved around, a few loyal customers followed him. One night, when a customer was told that it would take two weeks to fix his bike, Clott offered to bring his personal tools to the customer's office. "He was an accountant so I valued his business opinion, and I asked if he thought that I could make a business fixing bikes out of my truck. He said 'yes,' and so I went for it," said Clott.

Neil's note: Often your customer will tell you the business you should be in.

During the next six months, Clott worked seven days a week, 12 hours a day splitting his time between the bike shop and starting his own mobile repair business. At the end of the first year, Clott purchased a 22-foot box truck in which he built a complete bike repair shop. He figured out marketing. He set up a table at the top of Torrey Pines and handed out water and bananas to the riders as they crested the hill. People stopped, they talked, and if needed, they got a small adjustment to their bike. After Torrey, he expanded to other popular venues, and it has become his chief marketing tactic. He buys 20 dozen bananas a week.

(Neil's note: Marketing 101—Go to where your customer is.)

The next problem was how to scale. Clott teamed with a partner to buy a second truck. The deal fell through, and he learned an expensive lesson. "You can't create a business that is employee based. You have to create a business that is system based," he said.

Last year, Clott opened a physical shop in Kearny Mesa. The business currently has two full-time and one part-time employee, and Clott expects to generate $360,000 in revenue this year.

And here is Clott's clever financing strategy. He used credit cards that offer no interest during the first year. "I max out the cards, pay them off, and then cancel them. To open the shop, I got three cards on which I put $25,000," he said.

A tried-and-true entrepreneurial strategy—you can't beat zero percent interest.

His plans are to open a second shop and remain focused on service. (He does sell used bikes on consignment.)

Clott is the classic entrepreneur. He figured out how to meet a need, solve the problem and to do one thing really well. Most importantly, he had domain expertise because he had worked in the business for several years. We love the "little guy" who finds a place to stand, carves out his turf, defends it and ultimately builds a business.

Rule #364:
America needs to celebrate
the people who get their hands dirty—who make things.
Or in this case, fix them.

SAFETY NET CAN HELP ENTREPRENEURS GET OFF THE GROUND

November 17, 2014

Entrepreneurship is diverse across cultures, races, genders and politics. So, dear reader who may be more red than blue, please exercise restraint and caution.

Gareth Olds, an assistant professor at Harvard Business School, has found that a definitive link exists between new company formation and access to government assistance programs. "Having the net made these people more willing to walk on the high wire. It didn't make them want to walk on the net," says Olds.

The rate of new business births rose by 13 percent among households that qualified for State Children's Health Insurance Program, or SCHIP, and the survival rate of new businesses rose by 8 percent, according to Olds. In another study, Olds found a positive link between entrepreneurship and eligibility for the Supplemental Nutrition Assistance Program, or SNAP. Newly eligible households were 20 percent more likely to include an entrepreneur as a result of the policy and incorporated business ownership increased by 16 percent.

Not everyone who gets something from the government is a slacker or on the dole. And in this case, the facts speak for themselves—the true story of Oceanside business owner Jason Graves.

Graves, 38, an experienced telecommunications technician, had a run of bad luck. In 2010, he was laid off from his longtime job at the same time that he experienced financial difficulties coping with unexpected medical costs and problems with his insurance company related to a child's broken arm and fractured elbow. The combination ruined his credit rating.

"We burned through my severance and vacation pay. I cashed in my retirement account to start Green Air Lawn Care, a sustainable organic lawn care service and yard maintenance company in Oceanside," said Graves. To get started, Graves spent $10,000 for a truck, $2,500 for a lawn mower, $600 for a generator and several hundred dollars on shovels, rakes, clippers and a hose.

For many years, Graves had wanted to start his own business. "Amber (his wife) and I wanted to start something that had a moral compass that would make money and provide a feel-good for the customer." Green Air was a good fit because landscaping had been a longtime hobby. Since he had spent 20 years working inside in a cold refrigerated room, he welcomed the opportunity to work outdoors.

At the time, the Graves family included five children, all living at home. The family had no safety net, and as business revenues grew slowly, Graves applied for SNAP (food stamps) and Medi-Cal (for health insurance), programs that the family still uses.

"If it hadn't been for that help, we would have been living at a relative's house. No one is proud of being on his butt. I had spent 20 years working and paying into the system. My grandpa said never look down on a man unless you're trying to help him up. There is no doubt that these programs have given us the ability to reinvest money into the business that we wouldn't have been able to," said Graves.

To get his first customers, Graves printed up fliers and business cards, and he and his family went door-to-door in Oceanside. Now many new ones come from referral. Amber handles the office administration, and he employs one part-time contractor.

Recently, he borrowed money to upgrade his equipment from Accion San Diego, a nonprofit small-business lender primarily focused on helping low-to-moderate income business owners who lack access to traditional sources of credit.

Graves' story contains an important lesson.

Creating the opportunity to become self-sufficient is a core issue for the entrepreneur, and a helping hand, whether in the form of a mentor or in the form of financial support, is often necessary. Whether it is an SBIR (Small Business Innovation Research) grant to a scientist or food stamps to a lawn service, sometimes there really is a role for a government program. The entrepreneurial trapeze act is hard enough as it is, and having a touch of net at least lets you try without breaking your neck.

Rule #378:
That first step is a doozy.

INNOVATION HUB IN KEARNY MESA CUTS ACROSS AGES AND ETHNICITIES

August 23, 2011

Collaboration. Community. Campus. Connections. The Ansir Innovation Center, above the Tea Garden restaurant on Convoy Street between Engineer and Opportunity Roads in Kearny Mesa (talk about a Fortune Cookie address), is doing just that in creating the future of entrepreneurship in San Diego.

On a recent visit to the 7,000-square-foot, co-working and incubator space, we felt the energy, excitement and intensity as we met more than 30 entrepreneurs who were working in the open, flexible space. This is classic get down, no frills start-up space—just laptops and cords, couches, chairs and tables, and several small conference rooms. The place is decorated in a contemporary Asian influence in keeping with its founders Ping Wang, 32, and Bin Li, 29.

Wang and Li have created a private, for-profit incubator and co-working space with a clientele that cuts across all ages and ethnicities. (Think from dim sum to pizza.) Ansir is San Diego's answer to Plug and Play Tech Center and Y Combinator, two Silicon Valley incubators.

Describing his global view of the world, Wang said, "I was made in Taiwan, I grew up in Honduras, Texas and San Diego, where I graduated from Bonita Vista High School (valedictorian of course!)." Twenty-five years ago, Wang's father and uncle started Mytek International, a Tijuana manufacturing facility that has 1.5 million square feet set on 62 acres and produces more than 200 products.

After high school, Wang attended Stanford University, where he earned undergraduate and master's degrees in engineering, then returned to San Diego and got a Ph.D. in computational neuroscience from University of California San Diego.

Li moved from Fujian, China, to Bucks County, Pa., when he was in high school, and graduated from Penn State University. A job with Panasonic brought him to San Diego, where he earned a master's degree in global strategy and management from the University of San Diego. In 2008, he left the corporate world to start a consulting firm helping companies expand overseas.

Bridging the gap between San Diego and Asia will be a key driver to expansion capital, distribution and manufacturing.

Wang and Li met a few years ago, and last November came up with the concept for Ansir, which means "world harmony" in Mandarin. They had two goals: identify software that could be used in Mytek's products, and not work alone.

In less than 10 months, Wang and Li have created an innovation hub that is a water cooler for mentoring and connecting multiple start-up technology strands—software, clean tech, robotics and hardware.

So simple. And Wang and Li just did it perhaps because they didn't know any better.

"We wanted to create a humble environment in a multicultural setting where worlds could collide and connect, and next to some good food as well," Wang said.

Ansir offers:

- Co-working space starting at $100 per month.

- A series of mostly free educational programs such, as Hackaway Friday, featuring guest speakers; Coder Tuesday, at which developers code from 6 p.m. to midnight; and Hackathons focused on specific areas, such as mobile apps or government.

- Incubator services (for which Ansir takes an equity stake), including access to capital, manufacturing and design expertise for selected companies.

"Coming back to San Diego, I wanted to combine the Silicon Valley culture of innovation with the Asian culture of actually making things," Wang said. He believes that San Diego is rich in smart human capital and doesn't need to have Valley envy. He says that we have our own strengths, such as world-class universities and location next to Mexico.

The boys are not done. They plan to add 9,000 square feet in the building next door.

Theirs is not a bridge to nowhere. Their bridge extends west to Asia. And Asia wants to invest in the United States, but at this time in San Diego, "there is not a trusted partner that can cross cultural barriers. We want to be that trusted source and reach out to and engage global investors," Li said.

TAKING BABY BUSINESS STEPS CAN GET YOU FURTHER IN THE LONG RUN

May 19, 2014

Gimme a double mocha latte, nonfat espresso Frappuccino Macchiato and put them in 16-ounce cups to travel.

The coffee business is addictive but Elke Patton and her husband, Chuck, did not know that when she gave him a small coffee roaster for his birthday in February 2001.

Chuck liked drinking good coffee after living in San Francisco, where the couple had the opportunity to sample many different kinds. But liking coffee and starting a coffee business are as different as an Eskimo is to an Eskimo pie ice cream. And did I mention that Chuck did not have an MBA in anything? He was an English teacher at the local community colleges.

But remember Rule ##218: Grand passion and relentless pursuit will take you further than good grades. And Chuck was long on passion.

"The business evolved while I was teaching," said Chuck. "It started out as an after-hours business. I roasted coffee in the kitchen of the Veterans of Foreign Wars in Pacific Beach and sold it at the La Jolla farmers market. I started to understand the basic concepts of the coffee business such as the different kinds of beans, how to price and how to service wholesale customers. I learned gradually."

One year after getting the coffee roaster, Chuck quit teaching to formally start what has become Bird Rock Coffee Roasters, which specializes in offering quality coffee that he buys directly from the growers. The business operates one retail location in La Jolla, is opening another in the Little Italy area late this summer and also has a wholesale operation. In 2011, it was recognized as Micro Coffee Roaster of the Year by Roast magazine.

Meanwhile, Elke stayed at her position in a multinational, publicly traded financial-services company until last year, when she left to focus on growing the business. The go-slow, put your foot in one toe at a time is often a good way to start, and having one family member keep their job can provide much-needed stability in the throes of all the ups and downs of a startup.

Neil's note: Having only one member of the family deeply involved at the beginning adds longevity to a marriage.

As the business grew, Chuck subleased a retail space in a restaurant in the Bird Rock area of La Jolla and operated a kiosk in a grocery store parking lot. He also purchased a small wholesale business that owned a larger roaster. The one-step-at-a-time strategy.

Then in 2006, the Pattons took a big leap and opened the first Bird Rock Coffee Roasters independent retail location across the street from a Starbucks in La Jolla. Some people thought they were crazy to locate so close to the competition.

Neil's note: So you tell me, why are there often four gas stations on four corners? Because it works.

"When you're opening up across from Starbucks, people are already coming to that location to buy coffee so you don't have to change too many habits. It would have been harder if we were two to three blocks away," Chuck said.

A big plus in their favor was their knowledge of the community. They had lived five blocks away for 11 years, and both had been active in local organizations.

"The community saw the hard work that we were putting in, and so people gave us a shot. But we knew that people would only come back if the coffee was special. It is hard to compete against Starbucks, which does everything so well," he said.

Initial capital of under $75,000 came from putting a second trust deed on their house. At this point, I would argue they were "all in." Chuck wrote a simple business plan and sought advice from a

SCORE counselor. The couple purchased the building in which they started, and they have rented adjacent space as the business grew.

Starting a business can put a lot of stress on a marriage. Fortunately, Chuck and Elke recognized that they have very different skill sets. While Chuck focuses on the coffee (even traveling to visit the growers), Elke's strength is on the financial side. Since she is a former statistician who moved into product management, she is in charge of operations including technology, bookkeeping, human resources and insurance.

What keeps them up at night? "Our expansion plans, ensuring that we continue to source quality coffee, and to stay recognized on the national level. I want be one of the top five in the country," said Chuck.

Rule #355:
One step at a time is fine,
as long as they are all in the same direction.

WHAT IS A CULTURE AND HOW DO YOU CREATE ONE?
March 30, 2015

It has been said that culture is "a complex whole which includes knowledge, belief, art, morals, law and custom." Ok, I'll buy that, but how do you create one centered on innovation and invention when you have 31,300 employees in 198 world-wide locations. If you're Qualcomm, you innovate and invent your own. Meet the ImpaQt™ program. Launched in 2012, it is an initiative to empower all employees in all parts of the world to develop new product ideas within targeted areas. So far, over 10,000 people have participated.

"Ideas are cheap. What is important is execution. Our goal is to provide the right environment to take something from your head to something valuable in the market," said Navrina Singh, the head of ImpaQt. "We want the inventors to focus on their ideas and then my team can help them by identifying other team members and by providing the financial investment, the marketing and other resources to move the ideas forward."

A product that provides "surround sound" like quality on your mobile phone is now available thanks to ImpaQt and Robert Dessert, a senior product manager at Qualcomm. Dessert joined Qualcomm in 2008 after it purchased an Atlanta mobile commerce company where he worked. A few years later, he transferred to San Diego.

"My background was understanding credit card payments," said Dessert, who explained that his first career was in architecture and design. He said that he has never written a line of code. "One day I happened to stumble into the Qualcomm® Snapdragon™ room (a museum in honor of a Qualcomm Technologies, Inc. chip). I love music and I listened to a demo on headphones, and the sound was exactly like full 'surround sound' out of just standard headphones." He had an "aha" moment. "I thought why couldn't you create the surround sound experience on your mobile phone?"

In September 2013, Dessert submitted his concept to the ImpaQt program. The initial feedback questioned whether it was technically feasible. Still, his idea made it through the "Silent Auction," during which inventors are able to meet one-on-one with business unit leads and executives who are asked whether they will sponsor the idea. By enabling individual sessions instead of a group meeting, the ImpaQt program is providing every sponsor an equal weight in deciding which projects should move forward or be tabled.

The next steps are resource allocation (organizing a team with the necessary skills), building the prototype, showcasing the idea to the entire company and finally deciding whether to integrate the idea into an existing product, create a new product or shelve the idea completely. Just like in the start-up racket, sometimes things don't work out.

After his prototype was completed, Dessert and his team of three engineers pitched to a group of executives including Paul Jacobs, now Executive Chairman and formerly CEO of Qualcomm.

"I handed the phone to Paul, he hit play and listened to the demo. He couldn't believe it. He said Peter Chou (head of mobile phone giant HTC) needs to see this," said Dessert. "Two weeks later, my team and I flew to Las Vegas to meet with Peter, his COO, CFO and head of engineering. I gave the spiel again and handed the phone to him. They wanted it integrated into one of their upcoming devices right away.

Since March, it has been available on the HTC One M9.

In addition to delivering a stream of new products, ImpaQt provides participants with a deeper understanding of the product development process within a giant company.

"I learned that engineering is one small drop in the bucket of what it takes to build a successful product. Until I was involved with

ImpaQt, I didn't see product management and marketing in my daily job," said senior Qualcomm Labs engineer Zach Rattner, 24.

Engineer Ashwin Vijayakumar, 30, said the experience helped him gain people skills. "I learned the art of giving an elevator pitch to executives and business unit leads, in order get their buy-in for my proposal," he said. When he received feedback that his pitch lacked "oomph," he spent a weekend observing new car salesmen. "I noticed how they look us in the eye while talking, and they adjusted their pitch accordingly," he said.

Rule #395:
Cultured pearls of innovation are human creations
formed by inserting an idea into a benevolent medium.

CHILDCARE BUSINESSES SPRING FROM SOUTHWESTERN COLLEGE PROGRAM

January 22, 2013

The entrepreneur spectrum spans much more than high tech and biotech. For example, here is an entrepreneur who figured out child tech.

After years of struggling to make ends meet as a single mother, Julie Muñoz decided that she needed to change her life. And so she went back to school and learned a skill, one that is in high demand, cannot be outsourced to India and has a barrier to entry—her front door. In 2007, she graduated from Southwestern College's Microenterprise Family Childcare Program (MEFC), where she learned the competencies necessary to open a licensed child care business in her home. Today she runs Little Treasures Family Child Care, a thriving business with a waiting list of families wanting to use her services.

"Six years ago, I didn't think that I was worth anything. Now I know that I can do anything. I've been a good example for my 33-year old daughter and my grandson in middle school. At his school job fair, he saw my photo and he said, "My grandma has a successful business and some day I will be successful like her,' " said Muñoz, speaking in the child-friendly living room of her National City home. "I don't have to lay awake at night worrying about how to pay my bills. I have a new car in my driveway, and I'm able to do things with my grandkids."

Most importantly, Muñoz says she loves what she does. "This job is emotionally rewarding. You get hugs and kisses every day," she said.

She credits MEFC with teaching her to think like a business owner—not a baby sitter. In addition to child development and first aid, she learned about finance, taxes, bookkeeping and marketing. "When I get a new client, it starts with the first phone call because first impressions matter," she said.

This lady could go to the Valley and blow the doors down.

Her marketing efforts include handing out fliers at schools, preparing a 20-second elevator pitch for when people ask what she does, ads on Craig's List, and wearing a colorful "Little Treasures" T-shirt that says, "Quality child care at affordable prices, very kid friendly home with lots of TLC."

MEFC, which graduated its first class in 2006, counts 372 graduates of whom 76 percent have received a family child care license and 60 percent of whom are successfully operating a business one year after program completion. The 14-week program, which is offered twice a year, is free for the 30 participants and is funded by a grant from the U.S. Housing and Urban Development Department. The earning potential is from $36,400 to $54,600 a year based on four to six children and an average fee of $175 per week.

Most participants are women, and men are welcome although only a few have attended. Enrique and Maria Velazquez, an Oceanside couple, attended the class together and now operate a center with a large center license that allows them to serve up to 14 children. "When our daughter was born seven years ago, we couldn't find good quality child care, so when we heard about the Southwestern College, we decided to take the classes," said Enrique. "It felt strange because I was the only man with 29 ladies but after three weeks, it felt like a big family, and I was proud to be there."

The influence on the graduates can be enormous.

"I had no idea that it would have such a big impact emotionally, personally and practically on the participants. People tell us that now I have hope and a future. We are helping women to become economically self-sufficient, which results in an increase in their self-esteem and confidence," said Cynthia K. Nagura, director of MEFC and Southwestern's Family Resource Center.

There is no single rule for a moving story of success by bootstrap, of solving your own problem, and in so doing, solving the problems of many others. You cannot create an app that does childcare. We love the triumph of Muñoz and the Velazquez family for exactly that reason.

REFUGEES SHARE INSPIRING SUCCESS STORIES
January 21, 2012

Every once in a while, we find a story that embodies the triumph of the human spirit, the successful achievement against all odds, the individual passion for a better life that transcends all the noise from the digital, technology, blogosphere—just *mano-a-mano* against the darkness and the sadness. In this case, the manos are two women refugees whose stories give us all a moment to pause and consider our many blessings, particularly at this time of year.

Iraqi native Inas Khammi, 28, arrived in San Diego on Sept. 29, 2010. Speaking through an interpreter, she said her Chaldean Catholic family fled Iraq because of kidnapping threats due to their religion. In the U.S., she was eligible for $345 a month in cash assistance for eight months. Wanting to earn her own money, she looked at becoming a child-care provider to serve families in her community since she didn't speak English.

Her case manager told her about the WE Center for STAR Women, a partnership of Women's Empowerment International and the International Rescue Committee in San Diego that provides services to refugee and poor women who want to start or expand an existing business.

Lubna Saleem, a microenterprise business counselor whose salary is paid by WE, arranged for Khammi to attend child-care training in El Cajon, where she lives, in Arabic, and also helped her complete the application and coordinated the analyst home visit.

The STAR program also provided business management training and a $2,000 loan at 7.25 percent interest repayable over a two-year period so that Khammi could buy appropriate furniture and supplies. Khammi is current on her loan payments.

Today, Khammi's childcare business has a gross monthly revenue of $6,000. Her husband, Waad Gorges, (they met shortly after her arrival in San Diego) is proud that his pregnant wife is earning more money than he is. After their baby is born, they are planning to rent a bigger house and expand the day-care center. At that point, she will be eligible for another $15,000 loan. "I am much happier because we can buy what we want and have a comfortable life," said Khammi.

Another inspiring story is that is STAR Fashion, a small shop owned by another refugee woman, Fowsia Osman from Somalia. She sells scarves and shawls, jewelry and Somali garb.

Osman arrived in San Diego in 1998 when she was pregnant with her oldest son. Now a single mom, she has three sons—ages 13, 11 and 6. Through IRC, she learned English and attended child development classes, which allowed her to get a job with Head Start, where she worked for eight years. By 2007, she had saved $5,000, and with a $5,000 loan (which she has since repaid) and business assistance from STAR, she was able to open her shop.

Women's Empowerment International was started by two enterprising women—Winifred Cox, who had retired as director of communications for the University of California San Diego, and Leigh Fenly, who had retired as the "Quest" section editor with *The San Diego Union-Tribune*.

"Our goal is to help women build long-term sustainable businesses," said Cox. "We call what we're doing a business incubator because we're giving them one-stop shopping from idea through launch through growth and expansion. And you can always come back if you have a problem." Since inception in 2003, the WE organization, which has more than 700 members and supporters, has raised $540,000.

WOMEN'S EQUALITY FIGHT LONG, AND IT'S NOT OVER

April 16, 2013

In 1974, I was one of 107 women (15 percent of the class) entering the two-year MBA program at Harvard Business School 11 years after the first eight were enrolled alongside 676 men. Times do change.

A few weeks ago, 800 alumnae gathered at the W50 Summit to celebrate the past 50 years of women at HBS that was established in 1908. They came to share their experiences and challenges both at the school and during their careers, and most importantly, to engage in a dialogue on how the school can move forward in ensuring gender equality at the school and in the workplace.

But this is not just a Harvard story. The school's journey mirrors the journey of all women in the workplace over the last half century.

Harvard's retrospection on women is occurring at the same time that an intense conversation is taking place over Sheryl Sandberg's best-selling book, *Lean In: Women, Work, and the Will to Lead*. Sandberg, the chief operating officer of Facebook and HBS 1995, spoke to us about the themes of her book—that women are often held back because of their own insecurities ("keep your hand up because the world won't notice when you take it down"), our society's view of an ambitious woman as "distasteful," and the guilt that women often feel in trying to balance work and family.

Sandberg urged banning the words "having it all" from the English dictionary and noted that they are never applied to men. We need more women leaders, she said, because "Men still run the world, and I'm not sure it's going all that well."

HBS did a study on the history of women at the school and wrote a case (their preferred method of teaching), and it finds that over the last 50 years, sexism to various degrees has existed at the school. What a surprise.

As a student between 1974 and 1976, I felt awkward in a place that seemed to be focused on turning out investment bankers and consultants while I wanted to become a journalist or work on the business side of a publication.

While most of my classmates were never overtly hostile, a few male colleagues told me that I was only there to get a husband and that I was taking the place of a qualified man. During that period, women in other professional schools heard the same demeaning and derogatory comments.

At the same time, the school allowed me to create a class called Business and the Media. In this male-dominated environment, I was forced to learn important skills that have helped me through the many chapters of my life—to raise my hand, to be resilient after my divorce, to believe that I could succeed as an entrepreneur when I was in my 40s, and most importantly, to graduate determined to make it better for the next generation of women. That is why I started Athena San Diego, a professional and personal support network for women in the technology and life sciences community, and Run Women Run, an organization focused on electing more women to political office in San Diego.

HBS is in the business of educating future leaders, and how they tackle and solve these issues around women is important, because the school can help shape best practices and programs for women and men in all fields in our country.

After Sandberg spoke, HBS Dean Nitin Nohria concluded the summit by apologizing for the disenfranchisement that many of the women MBA students have felt over the years, and he pledged, "This is a long fight, and I'm in it for the long fight." With tears in our eyes, 800 of us stood to applaud his commitment.

Warren Buffett has said he "was privileged to work during a period when it was only necessary to compete against half of the population." That era has passed. Welcome to the other 50 percent.

Rule #176:
Gender equality is here to stay—
in business, in the military, in politics.
A woman may not necessarily "lean in"
but it's for sure she is going to hang in. And we will all be richer.

FEMALE PROFESSIONALS TAP COLLECTIVE WISDOM IN ATHENA

June 26, 2012

Finding a place for professional women to network 30 years ago was nearly impossible. As a female executive in the late 1970s and 1980s, I was sometimes the only woman in the room, and I was lonely.

In 1989, I was the associate director of Connect (an organization focused on nurturing technology and life-science entrepreneurs), and I began to see more women coming to our programs. So I thought, "There needs to be a place where women can help each other with their professional and personal challenges and issues."

And thus was born Athena San Diego. It has more than 500 members from our region's leading technology, life-science and health-care organizations and the service firms that support them.

I chose the name "Athena" because it was the name of a goddess of wisdom and war. She inspired and fought alongside the Greek heroes, and she was equal with the men. It sounded like the right combination of attributes for business success.

We began as an informal group of 25 to 30 women who met for lunch in a member's conference room. Telecom entrepreneur Martha Dennis hosted the first one. After a few years, our numbers grew too large to fit in a conference room, and we organized a few conferences. Then in 1997, when I left Connect to join a startup, I decided that Athena needed to become a formal organization if it were to grow and thrive.

To build a successful startup, whether it's in the nonprofit or for-profit sector, you need a great team with diverse skill sets. I was able to recruit an amazing group of 13 women to serve on Athena's first board of directors. We met several times over a one-year period to develop our original mission—"to unite senior women executives from high-tech and life-science companies, and the companies that support them, in a network that provides leadership, support and education, to address business issues and challenges unique to its members."

It has been almost 25 years since its inception, and I decided to talk with members about how Athena has helped them and whether they still see a need for a woman-focused organization. Men are welcome at Athena events, and generally about 20 percent of the attendees are very smart men!

(Neil's note: I was the first male member of Athena. It is not that the men were so smart, it was that they were involved with really smart and powerful women, and they needed to hang around with the big dogs.)

"I joined Athena because I wanted to learn from people whom I respected. There was so much that I didn't know. I gained friendships, advice, guidance, and a lot of perspective," said Tamar Elkeles, vice president of learning for Qualcomm and one of the founding board members. At the time, Elkeles was the youngest person in the room and was director of learning at Qualcomm. We all cheered her promotion to senior director and then to vice president.

Diane Goostree had moved from Kansas City to San Diego to become director of business development at a life-science company when she joined Athena in the early days. "I wanted role models so that I could understand how some women had risen in their careers and overcome obstacles, different pathways to success," said Goostree, who is now CEO of Intrepid Therapeutics. "Women tend to be more open with their thoughts and feelings, and I learned that no one is comfortable in a new role. If you are rising rapidly, you are doing new things all the time, and that causes some fear."

Erna Adelson, immediate past chair of the Athena board and senior director of information systems at Sony Network Entertainment, joined in 2006 when she moved to San Diego from

New Jersey. "I work in a male-dominated field, and I wanted to find other executive women like me who are driven and love the game of work and are focused on their career," she said.

Amylin accounts payable manager Kathy Tanner credits Athena and her FEW (Forum for Executive Women) group with helping her through her pregnancy and return to work. FEW is a group of eight to 10 Athena members who meet regularly in a confidential setting to discuss personal and professional issues and challenges. Tanner has also participated in Athena's one-to-one mentoring program and served on the committee that plans the annual Pinnacle Awards at which people and organizations that empower women are recognized and five female high school seniors who want to pursue a career in math or science fields receive scholarships.

WOMEN NEED TO BEAT DOWN THE DOORS TO GET TO THE TOP IN VENTURE CAPITAL

November 18, 2013

Having access to venture money is key to growing a high-value company, but the low number of female associates and partners in venture-capital firms makes it harder for female entrepreneurs because "they have a difficult time establishing connections that lead to investment," according to Gatekeepers of Venture Growth, a report published by the Kauffman Foundation.

In 2011, only 11 percent of the investment professionals at venture firms were women, says a survey by the National Venture Capital Association and Dow Jones VentureSource. The numbers have changed very little in the last 11 years.

However, female founders are finally making some progress. In 2004, female-founded companies represented only 4 percent of all U.S. venture deals compared with a record 13 percent of deals through the first half of 2013, shows data from PitchBook.

So what is the path for a woman to become a partner at a top venture capital firm?

For Kim Kamdar, a partner with Domain Associates, the journey started with a love for science that led her to Northwestern University, where as an undergraduate she "beat down the doors" of her professors until one allowed her to work in his lab.

Next she obtained a doctorate in biochemistry and genetics, and against the urging of her advisers (who wanted her to stay in academia and avoid "the dark side of industry"), she joined a pharmaceutical company that eventually became Novartis. As a young scientist at Novartis, she proposed a research project, secured funding from corporate headquarters in Switzerland, and was chosen to lead the team.

While visiting a Novartis affiliate in San Diego, she learned about the Kauffman Fellowship, a two-year program during which the participants work full time at a venture firm or another type of investment organization and also go through a structured curriculum tailored to their needs and interests. In 2003, Kamdar was accepted, and after she finished, she joined Domain as an associate in 2005, becoming a partner in 2011. Domain, started in 1985, focuses exclusively on the life-sciences sector and has raised more than $2.7 billion.

"When I was at Novartis, I thought that I was seeing a lot of technology and cutting-edge science. As a VC, I spend every day learning something new, and I get to work with people who are passionate about what they do and will do anything to get their technology and company off the ground," Kamdar said. Her scientific background combined with her operating experience at Novartis have been instrumental in analyzing deals and then working with companies as they grow, helping position them for a financing or acquisition or deal with a problem executive.

Although she is one of a few female venture partners, she said that she has never felt that being a woman was an obstacle. At Novartis meetings in Switzerland, she was often the only "fraulein" in the room in a formal culture where men were addressed as "herr," so she learned to stand up and be heard. Even recently, she said, she attended a meeting with partners from other venture firms, and she was the only woman out of about 40 participants. In contrast, three out of Domain's 10 partners are women compared with 18 percent for life-sciences venture firms in general, according to the NVCA survey. Clean-tech had 15 percent, followed by information technology at 12 percent and the lowest percentage was in the non-high tech products and services sector at 8 percent.

One of the biggest challenges in building a venture-capital career, she said, is that it takes a long time to figure out if you're any good. "If you're doing well, you should fail early, particularly in the life sciences, which requires long lead times and lots of money. So in the beginning you may have a lot of failures, and you have to learn to remain calm under duress," she said.

After gaining a solid foundation in science, Kamdar demonstrated curiosity, initiative, persistence and an ability to operate in diverse environments. Achieving success in venture capital is tough, and you need a unique set of skills and traits to become a partner at a major venture firm—a big accomplishment regardless of gender.

Rule #329:
Fail early and fail often,
but don't make it a habit.

LIFE AND DEATH CAN BE STRONG ENTREPRENEURIAL MOTIVATION

March 23, 2015

Rule #218:
Grand passion will take you further
than good grades.

And nothing focuses a passion more than when a problem is directly connected to your own life, as in living or dying.

Meet Laura Shawver. At the age of 49 in 2006, she was diagnosed with clear cell ovarian cancer. After getting the diagnosis, she was first surprised, then shocked and finally angry to learn that doctors had no idea what treatment to recommend for her particular case. This disease did not know who it was dealing with. Shawver was not your typical patient.

First, she has a Ph.D. in pharmacology, and second, she is relentless. She knew that a molecular profile of her tumor would help in determining the options, and she was upset that she could not easily get this done for ovarian cancer, even though it was being done regularly for patients with breast, lung and colon cancers.

After surgery, she underwent six rounds of chemotherapy while continuing to serve as chief executive officer of Phenomix, a San Diego biotech company that was raising $55 million in a financing. She scheduled her chemotherapy treatments around investor presentations. "I had chemotherapy every three weeks on a Wednesday, then I would take Thursday and Friday off, and go back to work on Monday. When we were in Boston and New York to pitch investors, my doctor would let me stay on steroids a day or so longer so that I wouldn't crash," Shawver said.

While dealing with her own situation, she decided to find a way to help others, so she started the Clearity Foundation, a nonprofit based in San Diego, in 2008 to help ovarian cancer patients and their physicians make better-informed treatment decisions based on the molecular profile of the tumor (the "tumor blueprint"). She chose the nonprofit route because she believed the number of new cases each year in the U.S. (about 22,000) weren't enough to interest a pharmaceutical company in focusing on the disease.

Clearity's goal is to help women find a more-individualized approach to therapy selection so they can live longer and healthier lives. The organization pays for the molecular profile of the tumor, recommends treatment options, maintains a database of patients and follows them so that over time it can provide better treatment recommendations. Even if Clearity cannot facilitate a molecular profile, they provide information about the disease, clinical trials and new drugs on the horizon.

"One of the barriers that we came up against is that physicians go through all the FDA-approved drugs, and only then do they think about a clinical trial or using a drug off-label. We need to shift that paradigm and bring a bolder, more creative approach," she said.

So far, more than 450 ovarian cancer patients have turned to Clearity for help. One of them is North County resident Liz Laats, 45, who was diagnosed with ovarian cancer five years ago. When she had a recurrence, she and her husband, Andy, went to see doctors all over the U.S.

"I could only get guesses from the medical establishment," recalled Laats, who is the mother of three children between the ages of 7 and 11. "After you have the first line of therapy and a period of remission, it comes back. Recurrence is a real problem, and treating it is a guessing game."

After registering on the Clearity Foundation website, Laats talked with one of the scientific advisers who explained more about her cancer and treatment options. "For the first time I felt that someone understood the situation that I was in, and that I wasn't just throwing darts. Chemotherapy works for a little while, and then you have to find the next one. You buy time, and hopefully better therapies come along."

As I've said, Shawver is relentless in her pursuit of a solution. After Phenomix closed up in 2010, she joined 5AM Ventures as an Entrepreneur in Residence and then became the CEO of Cleave Biosciences, based in Burlingame, driving their $54 million Series A financing. She is in the fortunate minority of ovarian cancer patients who have not suffered a recurrence.

She remains focused on growing Clearity's capacity so it can handle its 1,000th patient in three years, and in educating doctors, patients and insurance firms about the importance of individualized treatment plans. "The most expensive drug is the one that doesn't work," she said.

VISION, PERSISTENCE HAS LED ISIS CEO TO SUCCESS
February 3, 2014

Leading the development of a new platform technology for drug discovery, getting a drug approved by the Food and Drug Administration for a chronic illness and serving as chief executive of a company for 25 years are all significant accomplishments. Stanley Crooke, CEO and chairman of the board of Carlsbad-based Isis Pharmaceuticals, has achieved all three.

In 1989, Crooke started Isis to focus on antisense—a new technology that he believed could be used to create better drugs more effectively. At the time, he lived in the Philadelphia area, where he was the head of worldwide R&D at SmithKline Beckman, one of the world's largest pharmaceutical companies. He said that he located Isis in San Diego because it was one of three life-science centers in the U.S. (Boston and San Francisco were the other two), and he wanted to live here. Twenty-five years later, he is still the CEO of Isis, which has survived some tumultuous times when early research results were disappointing and cash was running low.

The firm has a market capitalization of about $5.5 billion and is trading at all-time highs largely because of the FDA's approval last year of Kynamro, a drug used to treat HoFH (a rare inherited condition that makes the body unable to remove "bad" cholesterol). The agency's action validates antisense as a proven, broadly applicable and efficient drug discovery platform. We caught up with Crooke to review the history of Isis.

Q: *Why did you want to start a company? Why couldn't you pursue antisense at SmithKline Beckman?*

A: I knew that developing a drug using antisense would take 20 to 25 years. You need a simple, focused agenda, and the agenda has to create a level of desperation. That desperation must be balanced by a commitment to do high-quality experiments. In a big company, 20 years is three CEOs, two mergers and 42 budget crises, so a high-risk long-term vision would eventually lose.

Q: *When did you know that antisense would work?*

A: It was 18 years and $2 billion before I became convinced that antisense would become a major drug discovery platform . . . Unless you're extremely lucky, all big ideas go through five phases—wild enthusiasm, disappointment, it will never work, grudging acceptance, and it was my idea to begin with. At Isis, we went through all of those phases.

Q: *How were you able to obtain the $3.8 billion that Isis has raised to date?*

A: If you have a big, high-quality dream and you appear to be a person who can realize that dream, it's possible to sell it and sell it again and weather the storms. (Crooke has been very savvy about financing. Isis went public in 1991—very early in its existence—and quickly did secondary offerings when market conditions permitted. Other funding has come from additional equity investment, license fees and royalties. Isis had $625 million in cash at the end of 2013.)

Q: *How did you handle the disappointments? (The company had two products that failed in late-stage clinical trials.)*

A: The senior people and I looked at the data and said do we see a path forward? Every time we looked we did see a path, and every step took us closer to a success scenario. At times it wasn't clear that we would be able to raise the money to continue. There was tremendous depression because of the disappointment and tremendous fear and anxiety in the organization that had to be managed and marshaled to a new enthusiasm. The key to leading through a crisis is to pivot to a new dream that is consistent with the overall dream.

At a major turning point, Crooke turned to his wife, Rosanne Crooke, one of the key scientists at Isis, and asked her to lead the team that developed Kynamro. "We're best friends and partners. We manage disappointments by looking forward, we try to be upbeat and focus on the positive and learn from our mistakes," said Rosanne.

Rule #218:
Grand passion and relentless pursuit
will take you further than good grades.

LAMENT OF THE CEO: I WAITED TOO LONG
November 10, 2014

If you put 100 chief executives in a room and asked them, "What is the biggest mistake you have made?" I believe that 99 of them would answer, "I waited too long."

This truth is inviolable. It is a proven statistic. And it saddens me, because "clock management," whether on the football field or in the boardroom, matters a great deal. Running out of time is the sin most closely related to running out of money.

Maybe they waited too long to hire, to fire, to kill a product, to launch a product. It doesn't matter—they waited too long.

A CEO I know well comes to see me. He needs money, cannot meet payroll, and would like an investment—in a week. He knows and I know that is not going to happen. But I wonder why it took him so long to come and see me.

Another company comes to see me. They need a $2.5 million bridge loan for 90 days, and they think they can arrange a management buyout during that time, which is probably unrealistic. The venture capitalists will not put in any more money, and the company will run out of money in two weeks. How does it come to this? Here is the handwriting on the wall. One of the venture capitalists in the deal had not been to a board meeting in 18 months. If you want money in two weeks, then the crush-cram-down is coming. So the benefit the CEO wants, which is to salvage his company, is effectively taken away by the cost of the money he is seeking.

And then he wonders why the money is vulture money. It is vulture money because you waited too long to go looking for it, and let's be honest, that investor is not your Uncle Harry, he is not your friend. To quote from *The Godfather*, "It's not personal, Sonny, it's strictly business."

This story can be told and retold in myriad ways. So why is it so hard to see down the road. To explore this issue, we turn once again to my favorite Nobel Prize winner, Dan Kahneman, for his work with Amos Tversky on "prospect theory."

Kahneman's study focuses on behavioral economics. He proves that people are risk-averse when facing gains and risk-seeking when facing losses. This finding is in direct contradiction to traditional economic theory that posits that people will always behave rationally and pick the optimum solution when facing a gain or a loss.

When it comes to raising money for the company, the reason entrepreneurs wait too long is that they fear dilution, they fear loss of control, they fear embarrassment, they fear regret, and they fear the price to be paid for salvation. Recently, a man came to us and admitted his company was dead meat, and he asked if we would buy it in an asset sale. We said yes and wanted the CEO to come with it. We talked to one of the venture capitalists who backed the company originally. He told us that he would not sell for less than $10 million, and they were going to put in more money. In other words, he told us to drop dead. One month later, the company closed. I guess he showed us who's boss. The VC has pride, and he also has the pleasure of losing other people's money.

People consider losses twice as painful as gains, but having to acknowledge the loss, to actually take the loss, to have to lower your expectations and hopes and dreams—well, people do not like to do that—and they wait too long. Kahneman says, "That is why in the stock market, most people sell their winners and hold on to their losers. They want to believe that they will come back."

I will add one equally important corollary to the "don't wait too long" theory. That is "do not leave a mess." Do not run the company to zero and not make the final payroll. There is personal liability in that scenario. Do not leave creditors with nothing. Before the final bell, offer a settlement and act honorably. The wheel is always spinning. You will meet them again. Just like your mother said, "Do the dishes and clean up your room, Johnnie." And what is fascinating is that studies show that we believe these errors in thinking only affect other people, not us.

Rule #347:
Look in the mirror.

BEING SHOWN THE DOOR HURTS BUT EXIT GRACEFULLY
February 17, 2014

Rule #115:
Do you want to be rich or do you want to be king?
If you choose the latter, you are doomed to failure.

I turned in my crown 20 years ago.

In two days, I will be fired as CEO of my alternative fuel company. This will be the second time over eight companies that I have been removed. I think it "comes with the territory."

I read the other day that the CEO of Living Social is "stepping down." Stepping down, spending more time with family, personal reasons, the company needs someone to take it to the next level—it doesn't matter what you call it, you are getting tossed.

If you want a friend, get a dog.

I founded the company three years ago, took it a long way, raised over $20 million, built the first working plant of its kind in North America, created partnerships, and made good deals. But at the end of the day, my financial partner decided he could run it better than I could. And you all know the golden rule.

The reason I am sharing a personal story is that it is always easy to give advice about not being depressed and something else will appear etc., but when the person you are giving that advice to is you—well, "physician, heal thyself."

This entrepreneur thing is hard, and the CEO thing is even harder. Statistically, more than 52 percent of startup chief executives get fired within the first three years. I started this company in December 2010, so I am right on time.

And while I am looking in the mirror, I will remind you of one more axiom. As CEO, do not expect the company to thank you. I know you worked hard, made the best decisions you could for the team, created jobs, provided health care, built a strong culture. Don't let the door hit you on the way out. No thank yous. The people staying with the company need the job and need the money. No one follows you off the Coronado bridge.

The assignment now is to exit gracefully and make the best deal that you can.

Two days later in a law office in Carmel Valley

The boys flew in on their jet. They could not have been nicer. Turns out they did fire me but they asked me to stay on the board and help out for the next year or so. Reasonable men and a reasonable outcome. Even some laughter, and I almost liked their lawyer.

And now, as I prepare to exit stage left, here are some sobering thoughts from my favorite Harvard professor, Noam Wasserman. His research shows "that the most successful of founders, the ones who led their startups to completing key milestones the quickest, were actually the first ones to get fired."

Wasserman calls this "the paradox of entrepreneurial success." When you are the creator of the company, "you're increasing the chances that you are going to get fired."

You start the company, and you raise money. Then you have investors and a board. Wasserman says, "When you have lost control of the board, and the next stage of growth is on the horizon, the chances of getting fired are heightened dramatically."

Here is the kicker that makes me feel great: "Founders who keep control of their boards and hang on to the CEO position, their personal equity wealth ends up being half as much, as if they give up control to a brand-new CEO with resources to grow the company," according to Wasserman.

I remain a large stockholder and a big supporter. I feel so good about being tossed, I think I will go out and test-drive a Tesla.

ILLUMINA CO-FOUNDER FINDS PASSION IN SCIENCE FESTIVAL

April 7, 2014

"Illumina named world's smartest company," said the MIT Technology Review's annual list of really brainy and smart companies. Facebook did not make the cut, but Google did, finishing third behind Tesla.

And in case you were not aware, Illumina was co-founded by one of our all-time favorite people: entrepreneur, venture capitalist and philanthropist Larry Bock.

But if you asked him what he is most passionate about, it would not be the more than 40 companies that he has funded, started or helped (with a cumulative market capitalization in excess of $40 billion according to his bio).

It would be the USA Science & Engineering Festival that is expected to attract more than 250,000 people over the April 26-27 weekend in Washington, D.C.—the culmination of a yearlong program of events. Bock says this makes it the largest STEM (science, technology, engineering and math) outreach event in the world.

"As a society, we get what we celebrate. We celebrate athletes, pop stars and Hollywood actors and actresses, but we don't celebrate science and engineering. So why not have the largest celebration of science and engineering in the U.S., and that's what we endeavored to create," Bock said.

Bock is an indomitable force full of unlimited energy. When he decides to tackle a project, nothing can stand in his way. The idea for the first science festival originated when Bock and his family visited a science festival in Cambridge, England, and he was so excited about the concept that he decided to create one in San Diego.

According to an article on **inewsource.org**, he put up $150,000 in seed capital and raised $550,000. His goal was to attract 15,000 attendees, so he was astounded when more than 100,000 people came to the inaugural San Diego event in Balboa Park in 2009.

After this success, he worked with UC San Diego to obtain a five-year, $3 million grant to expand the science festival, and he agreed to donate $200,000, plus his time.

Frustrated with the red tape, he turned his focus on developing a national event in Washington. Locally, the nonprofit Biocom Institute puts on the San Diego Festival of Science & Engineering—the latest one took place last month.

Like any entrepreneur, Bock is continually striving to make improvements. Most importantly, he said, the Washington event is now year-round with programs like the 150 "Nifty Fifty" science and engineering professionals who speak about their work and careers at various middle and high schools and the biannual series "Lunch with a Nobel laureate."

With the theme "Getting Science Right in Hollywood," he has recruited science consultants from TV series like "Breaking Bad," "House" and "The Big Bang Theory."

Other participating celebrities include basketball legend Kareem Abdul-Jabbar, the author of *What Color is My World?: The Lost History of African-American Inventors*, and Miss California Crystal Lee. Lee will talk about the importance of encouraging more women to pursue STEM careers. She is a second-generation Chinese-American who graduated from Stanford University with a B.A. in marine biology and an M.A. in communications a week before earning the Miss California title in 2013.

This year, a large number of exhibits will focus on new manufacturing technologies like 3-D printing.

"These technologies will lead to the democratization of manufacturing, letting anyone build a product from scratch. One of our participating companies—Shapeways—is literally offering over 90,000 products from small inventors," he said.

Bock is a man of grand passion and stands as the epitome of an entrepreneur who has given back and whose life demonstrates how one person can make a difference. And he is not standing still.

He wants STEM to be mainstream, to be what cool kids want to learn and embrace. As he puts it, "We will be happy when ABC's 'Good Morning America' has as much coverage of a science festival as they do of Comic-Con."

Rule #348:
Leave footprints. Make a difference.
Life is short.

B LAB NOTES COMPANIES WITH CONSCIENCE
June 17, 2013

It is one thing to do good and do well. But it is quite another to tell your investors up front that not all the profit actually goes to them. In prior columns, we have written about our support of the nonprofit entrepreneur with a commitment to social enterprise. Now, a new twist in the for-profit arena has come along, and its premise is transparency to your investor of your intention that you are concerned about more than making money for them. It is called a "B Corporation," and it requires that your company be certified by the nonprofit B Lab that independently verifies rigorous standards of social and environmental performance, accountability and transparency. In that way, you can do good and do well, and your investors know the score going in.

The emphasis on metrics in addition to profits has not hindered some of these "B" companies from raising big money—Warby Parker ($55 million), **Change.org** ($15 million), and Etsy ($91 million).

In San Diego, B Corporation Mamma Chia has raised several million dollars primarily from angel investors, said Janie Hoffman, the founder and CEO. The company makes organic chia-based food and beverages that use the chia seed, a grain that contains omega-3, antioxidants, protein and fiber. The products are sold in Whole Foods, Von's, Ralphs and other retailers.

"Our investors are aligned with our mission. Having the certification was positive for them," said Hoffman. "So many companies say that they're doing something good for the environment and the community when they're not, which is why the independent B certification is great."

Like all B Corporations, Mama Chia's rating of 88 points (out of 200) is available on the B Lab website. Eighty points is the minimum required to earn the certification. The four metrics that compose the rating are:

- Governance: mission, stakeholder engagement and overall transparency of the company's policies and procedures

- Workers: compensation, benefits, training, ownership and work force environment

- Community: supplier relations, diversity and community involvement

- Environment: facilities, resource and energy issue

From the beginning, Mamma Chia has donated 1 percent of gross sales to support local food systems, more than 20 percent of suppliers are local and are located in low-income communities, and 50 percent of office supplies come from recycled/sustainable materials.

Another certified B Corporation with San Diego roots is Warby Parker, which was started in 2010 to create boutique-quality, classically crafted eyewear at an affordable price point. David Gilboa, one of the four founders, graduated from Torrey Pines High School in 1999 and met his three co-founders when he was earning his MBA at the Wharton School at the University of Pennsylvania.

"We were frustrated at the high cost of prescription glasses that can cost $300 or more," said Gilboa. "A few big companies controlled the $65 billion industry. We thought that by creating our own brand, dealing direct with manufacturers and consumers, we could disrupt the industry by cutting out the middle men and sell glasses to consumers for $95, including the lenses."

As the son of two doctors, Gilboa said he always wanted to work in a field in which he could earn a paycheck and provide a social benefit. Seeking the B Corporation certification made sense because "as operators and owners, we want to be held accountable for actions that take into account all of our stakeholders such as employees, customers and the environment at large. In the traditional corporation, the only interests that you have to protect are the shareholders'," Gilboa said.

Almost 1 billion people worldwide lack access to glasses, so Warby Parker has partnered with nonprofits to ensure that for every pair of glasses sold, a pair is distributed to someone in need.

"Our investors (the company has raised $55 million) are very supportive of how we're building the business and the resources and capital that we're using to further the development of our employees and to buy carbon offsets," said Gilboa.

The B certification is in addition to whatever legal structure a company chooses. "Any type of legal form (LLC, LLP, or C Corporation) can become a B Corporation," said Susan H. Mac Cormac, a partner in the San Francisco office of Morrison & Foerster.

Only 760 companies have achieved B Corporation certification since it was offered beginning in 2007, according to B Lab spokesman Andy Fyfe, who said that more than 7,000 companies are using the assessment tool to benchmark themselves. "It is difficult to pass the bar. These companies are competing to be the best in the world and for the world," he said.

Rule #241:
To B or not to B, that is the question.

SOCIAL CHANGE, NOT PROFIT, IS WINNING INNOVATOR'S AIM

May 15, 2012

For a certain breed of entrepreneur, the next big thing is not always about money. It is about applying their skills to find sustainable and innovative ways to change the world and make it better, and the University of San Diego is taking a lead role in this important trend with its recent Social Innovation Challenge competition.

This year's winner, Eat Better Today, is a mobile food-catering truck that will provide healthy food to homeless individuals. Eat Better Today's founder Teresa L. Smith, who is studying for a master of arts degree in nonprofit leadership, beat out 51 other teams for the $10,000 first-prize award. The service will begin in late May, and the homeless will be able to pay with Cal-Fresh benefits (formerly known as food stamps).

Before starting the masters' program at USD, Smith was already an entrepreneur in the nonprofit sector. A trained social worker who has long been involved with homeless issues, in 2009 she started Dreams for Change to "utilize innovative techniques and methods to meet the basic needs" of the homeless. The organization's first initiative was the Safe Parking Program that provides a supportive environment for homeless who live in their cars. Next came food.

"I got the idea for Eat Better Today a little over a year ago when I was talking to some of the participants in the Safe Parking Program. They talked a lot about the food issue—waiting in long lines, getting food that wasn't great or healthy, and of course they don't have a place to prepare their own meals," said Smith.

Just like any entrepreneur, Smith listened to her customers. This is a core principle in the "lean startup" model. The customer will tell you what business you should be in. Listen to them.

Keeping costs down was important, so Smith worked with

the county of San Diego to be able to accept Cal-Fresh benefits and to enroll people seamlessly at the truck. The county has provided funding for a worker to handle the applications. The Uptown Rotary Club and the Lions Club have also provided capital. In essence, she built a socially focused support network where each element provided a small piece of the puzzle, and no one organization bore the whole burden.

In addition, Smith said, "We will be using a lot of volunteers to make the food and work on the truck, and we are asking the homeless to volunteer so they learn about how to run a small business. We want to empower them." The group has purchased a used food truck for $26,000, and Smith estimates that the annual cost of operating one truck is $100,000. Her goal is make each truck self-sustaining through the revenues from Cal-Fresh.

Smith credits the USD master's program with being an important source of inspiration. "I've learned that you have to be willing to take risks. People told me there is no way you can pull this off. It's too far out there. I learned that when you're pushing the envelope of change, this is a standard response. I've also learned that failure is all right and that you have to be able to move to the next stage," she said.

"Social innovation requires energy, creativity and enthusiasm, having your feet on the ground and a willingness to do the hard work," said Patricia Marquez, director of USD's Center for Peace and Commerce, which is collaboration between the School of Business Administration and the Institute for Peace and Justice.

Note: While USD celebrated social innovation, the annual University of California San Diego's Jacobs School of Engineering Research Expo featured "posters" by 230 graduate students, many of whom also have entrepreneurial dreams. The winner—Carolyn Schutt, a Ph.D. student in bioengineering—is developing a more sensitive imaging technique that can hopefully improve how we diagnose breast cancer. Schutt also finds time to participate in the community. She was the lead organizer for the Jacobs School exhibit at the recent San Diego Festival of Science and Engineering for K-12 students.

Our city is alive with the sound of innovation.

Rule #52:
If you can do well at the same time you do good—
that is the next big thing.

HOORAY FOR HOLLYWOOD MOVIES ABOUT BUSINESS
July 22, 2013

When I was younger, I worked as a writer in Hollywood. The business of Hollywood is not a business. It makes the used-car industry look like the nuns of Santa Lucia. And picking winners—impossible. The most famous quote about Hollywood comes from William Goldman (Oscar winner for the script of *Butch Cassidy and the Sundance Kid*), who once said, "Nobody knows nothing."

But one thing Hollywood does know is how to make movies about business. And let's take a look at a few older movies and see what their stories can teach us and how they resonate with us today.

Citizen Kane, directed by Orson Welles, is based loosely on the life of newspaper magnate William Randolph Hearst. In the movie, Welles has a famous line: "You're right. I did lose a million dollars last year. I expect to lose a million dollars this year. I expect to lose a million dollars next year. You know, Mr. Thatcher, at the rate of a million dollars a year, I'll have to close this place—in 60 years."

So this is the school where Tumblr, Groupon, Facebook, Pinterest, Zynga, etc. got their MBAs. This is the beginning of the "profits, we don't need no stinking profits" mantra that has infected some contemporary technology startups. The difference, of course, is that Hearst had very deep personal pockets, no board of directors, and did not have to go public to get liquid.

Wall Street, starring Michael Douglas as an amalgam of Michael Milken, Ivan Boesky, and a host of other "masters of the universe," has the famous line, "Greed is good."

Not anymore. The rise of nonprofits and the desire by the new technorati "to both do well and do good" belie that hoary line. Google's corporate motto was "don't be evil." One can debate whether that is the case today or not, but at a minimum, it was originally well intentioned.

The Godfather, starring Marlon Brando, has the signature line, "I'm going to make him an offer he can't refuse." This remains a brilliant tactical model for negotiation—sans guns. Understanding the chess board and placing your opponent in a position where there is only one outcome is difficult but compelling. It requires standing in the other person's shoes (not cement) and then playing the game until you are one move from checkmate—and then of course, an offer he cannot refuse.

The other great line from *The Godfather*, among many, is "Leave the gun, take the cannoli." I offer no deep thoughts on that one except that I love the cannoli at Bussalachi's restaurant in Hillcrest.

Jerry McGuire, starring Tom Cruise, is a story of loyalty and perseverance in a world where "the key to this business is personal relationships."

I think this is critical in doing deals—and it argues for what I call doing "road work." This means get on a plane and go see the client, the customer, the deal guy—you have to be in his face, breaking bread. The Internet lets you do WebEx and everything else short of pressing the flesh, but the truth is, you need to sit across from someone. And of course, "Show me the money."

In startup terms, that means do not waste time with pretenders or prevaricators or promoters. Find the guy who actually writes the checks.

Glengarry Glenn Ross tells you everything you will ever need to know about selling. ABC—Always Be Closing. "First prize is a Cadillac Eldorado. Second prize is a set of steak knives. Third prize is you're fired." What more is there to say? No pitch decks, no power points, no excuses. It is the win/lose finality brought down to simple basics for your company.

I love movies about business. They inform us in ways that TechCrunch (a technology blog) never will. And when we see courage, passion, perseverance, and triumph, we applaud even if along the way a couple people have to take the fall.

LOOKS MATTER, BUT BUSINESS SAVVY IS MORE IMPORTANT

April 14, 2014

Today's column is a bouillabaisse. That is a $26 word that suggests I am going to throw everything into the soup, heat it up and hope you don't get sick.

First, as you know, Ms. Bry and I are big supporters of smart female entrepreneurs. However, it seems we are in the minority. A team of researchers from MIT, Harvard, and Wharton has done a study that indicates strongly "that venture capitalists prefer to back entrepreneurial opportunities when pitched by a man."

OK, I get it, nothing new there. But the next sentence in the study might flatten you a bit. "They are more likely to offer funding if the man is good-looking." The paper was published in March in the *Proceedings of the National Academy of Sciences*.

So, now I know why it is so hard for most of us to get venture financing—we don't look like Brad Pitt. And to top this off, the study indicates that it doesn't matter if the woman pitching the deal is good looking.

Huh, you mean to tell me you wouldn't fund Scarlett Johansson even if she were pitching online pet food? (If she were delivering the stuff personally, she could get a $100 million pre-money, and Kleiner Perkins and the boys in the Valley would fund without a blink.)

The study is detailed and has lots of percentages and impressive calculations, but at the end of day, the conclusion is that beautiful men do better in getting investment dollars than average men, as well as all categories of women, gorgeous or otherwise. If you want a link to the study, send us an email.

Second, over the past few weeks, my partners and I have seen a variety of deals, and one theme emerges clearly. The entrepreneur needs to "answer the question being asked." We had an instance in which an entrepreneur gave a series of fuzzy answers to some direct questions.

As the pitch ended, I suggested to the entrepreneur that there were only two possible answers—one, the correct and true and honest one, and two, it is OK to say, "I don't know." The rule here is a simple one. I have a Ph.D. in bull—-. I teach the course in that subject, so do not try to bull—- me. It detracts from your credibility. It is OK to not know the answer, just be willing to say so.

Next, you have to get the easy things right the first time. We see a lot of deals in which the founder comes in, and we are interested. In probing further, we find that there is "hair on the deal"—meaning that there are some basic mistakes that need to be fixed—like the corporate structure, valuation at first funding from friends, vesting, co-founder issues.

This is basic stuff that should never get in the way of advancing your company. And the sad sentence is that fixing is always harder than getting it right in the first place. Fixing means there are going to be uncomfortable conversations, so why create brain damage if you don't have to?

Last week, we had a pitch from some very smart young men (and attractive as well), but when I asked them the infamous rich vs. king question, the three of them flunked it unanimously.

I know the founder has the vision, the passion, the desire, etc., but let me tell you, being CEO is overrated. It is a very tough, often miserable job. If you can get someone better than yourself, then do it. Be the founder, own the most stock and let someone else wage the daily wars—particularly someone who has done it before in your domain.

Recently, we were willing to fund a young genius, and at the final interview, he asked me if he could make the "business decisions." I said, no, not in the beginning. He was a technical genius, but in my opinion had only modest business skills.

He said he wanted to learn and that it was important for him to make the business decisions. In other words, he wanted to learn on my investment.

If he really wants to learn the business side, then he should go back to school—but why do that when it's better to get a co-founder with those skills?

Rule #349:
The entire world of entrepreneurship is encapsulated
in the Seinfeld "Soup Nazi" episode.
Watch it again.

IT'S NOT SO EASY BEING KING IF YOU ALSO WANT TO BE RICH

May 29, 2012

Do you want to be rich or do you want to be king? This is one of the first questions that we ask an entrepreneur. If the founder answers "king," the meeting is over.

King means that you want to sit on the throne and maintain control as the CEO and owner. Rich means that as the company grows, you're willing to give up the throne and bring in a new CEO and outside investors. Think about it. Would you rather own 0.01682 percent of Google or 93 percent of Manny's Deli?

Yes, you can point to Bill Gates, co-founder of Microsoft, and Irwin Jacobs, co-founder of Qualcomm, and now Mark Zuckerberg of Facebook. All of them kept the CEO role and a great deal of stock as their companies grew. But they are the exception. Most of us are not in their league.

In his new book, *The Founder's Dilemmas*, Harvard Business School professor Noam Wasserman has collected an astounding amount of data on the rich v. king question and other key issues that high potential (mostly technology and science based) startups encounter. In examining 460 startups, for example, he found that "founders who keep control personally give up a significant amount financially. Such founders tend to build a less-valuable startup."

And listen to this: "Founders who kept control of both the CEO position and the board of directors held equity stakes that were only 52 percent as valuable as those held by founders who had given up both the CEO position and control of the board." In other words, if you rule the roost, your chicken coop is worth half of that of a competitor who did not have complete control. Wasserman points out that first-time founders don't understand the various stages of growth, they don't realize that those stages will pose different challenges to the CEO, and they don't yet know whether they have the skills to deal with the issues.

Rule # 217:
It's what you don't know that you don't know
that will kill you.

Last September, we met Wasserman at Barbara's Harvard Business School reunion, and we were impressed at the research that he has conducted on why startups succeed and fail and how to avoid common mistakes. His book should be required reading for all entrepreneurs. And on the subject of replacing the CEO, Neil can tell you that the board of directors fired him as CEO from his first software company, and it was sold one year later for over $100 million to Cisco.

An important issue into which the book delves is who makes the best co-founders—friends, family, strangers or co-workers? What Wasserman found is that "co-founders with prior social relationships are often the least likely to deal with the elephants in the room." Our personal corollary to that, however, is that founders who work with people they have worked with before have a higher success rate. The key difference is social versus business.

For example, Apple co-founders Steve Jobs and Steve Wozniak were good friends before they started the company, and later they "failed to discuss crucial issues about roles and rewards that were too uncomfortable for best friends to broach." And of course, after a couple of years, Woz left Apple.

What we like about Wasserman is that his evidence is empirical. He mined quantitative data from almost 10,000 founders. The result is clear and somewhat painful. You might start out as the founder genius, but your chance to be really rich is exponentially increased if you give up the lead reins. The trick in that puzzle is knowing the right time to do that and to whom.

FINDING RIGHT CO-FOUNDER IS KEY TO "HAPPY MARRIAGE"

August 15, 2013

How many technology companies with a market cap greater than $5 billion were started by a single person—in other words without a co-founder?

That's right. The number is zero. (Bloomberg doesn't count—it is finance.)

The "charismatic faces of the company" quickly come to mind—think Bill Gates, Larry Ellison, Steve Jobs, Mark Zuckerberg, Mark Andressen, et al. All of them had a co-founder. You need at least one other person for myriad reasons, from financial to psychological to technical.

A co-founder is different from Employee #1. This is the person with whom you "create" the company—i.e. the one with whom the idea is germinated, agreed upon, and initiated. True, the company will morph and pivot countless times, and your co-founder is part of that process.

Let's talk money, stock, and wealth. When you start your company, a co-founder will get between 10 percent to 30 percent of the company. In some cases, maybe even 50-50—although in general I strongly oppose that split. You cannot be co-chief executives—never, ever, no way, no how. One person almost always brings more value. (As you can see, I do not feel strongly on this issue.)

In addition, I am advising both of you to have vesting agreements and a "prenup," because this is a marriage, and many marriages end in divorce. And you do not want a lawyer giving away your mother's antique rocking chair.

Read Zuckerberg v. Saverin. Also read Zuckerberg v. Winklevoss. The law firms of Silicon Valley and New York are littered with "disagreements."

Now finding the right co-founder ranks right up there with finding a spouse. Not so easy. Ironically, the Internet has begun to address the problem with websites devoted to helping you find this one magic person—sort of a **Match.com** for founders, (e.g. Founder2Be, FounderDating). However you find your true love, here are some things to consider.

Complementary skills: No baseball team needs four shortstops and zero outfielders. If you write code, you need a Wharton/Harvard dropout or an MBA and vice versa.

Mutual respect: Do you really like being around this person? You better, because you are going to be around him or her 24/7 for the first year.

Shared goals: One of you wants to cure cancer in Africa; the other wants a Gulfstream 6. Get in sync.

High degree of flexibility: This calls for fiercely embracing the infamous "rational man behavior" mantra. No neurotic co-founders.

The Startup Genome Project says that "balanced teams with one technical founder and one business founder raise 30 percent more money, have 2.9 times more user growth and are 19 percent less likely to scale prematurely."

Lastly, when do you start to look for a co-founder? The answer: Before you have a firm idea. That's right, because you are looking for a co-founder, not employee #1. You are looking for someone to be part of the getting pregnant, not someone to just deliver the baby or be the nanny.

Dig the well before you need the water. Avoid desperation and the leaping into the arms of the first person who says yes.

I love partners/co-founders. I have never done anything, from Hollywood to real estate to technology, without a partner. I know what I don't know, and I proactively seek out the ying to my yang. The startup adventure is a tough road regardless, and it always better to have someone else in the car just in case you fall asleep at the wheel.

Rule #267:

If you have a co-founder,
at least you won't have to eat lunch alone.

OWNING A BUSINESS WITH SPOUSE CAN BE CHALLENGING, REWARDING

November 4, 2013

Rule #328:
Even if it is a small ship,
you are still the captain.

So you've had it up to here and you want to tell "the Man to take a hike, pound sand and, by the way, I am outta here." Making a successful transition from a large organization to owning your own small business can be treacherous.

Suddenly you are the ultimate decision-maker operating without the safety net of a regular paycheck and easy-to-access help for everything from fixing a broken computer to cleaning the bathroom. The situation poses major changes and challenges both for you and your family. And if you decide to do this "together with my spouse," be aware that marital strife can be exacerbated by aggravation at the office.

In 2004, after 25 years in corporate America, Paul Jester decided it was time to own a business. Although he had spent a number of years working for startup technology companies, including the successful HNC Software, he decided to look for something low-tech because he didn't "want to look over my shoulder and wonder what new technology was going to bite me on the ass."

Jester followed our Rule #2: "Networking is a profession, become a professional at it," and he started by talking with numerous business owners in a variety of sectors. This led to a conversation with a sign company owner. Jester decided that he liked the business—the fabrication part particularly appealed to his engineering background.

Through further research, he identified an 8-month-old company that he was able to buy for $75,000—more than the liquidation value and less than it would have cost to replicate. Meet the proud owner of Miramar Sign Works & Graphics.

Next, he spent an additional $35,000 to join Signworld, an organization of more than 260 sign owners that provides training and support as well as a forum in which the individual owners can post questions and share best practices. This was a smart move because often you don't know what you don't know but you have to be willing to take a leap.

"I didn't know anything about signs, but I knew how to sell," said Jester. "When someone asked if I could make a particular type of sign, I always said 'yes, absolutely.' Then I would ask for advice on the Signworld forum."

For the first 18 months, cash flow was tight, and Jester dipped into savings to keep the business operating. As he looked around, he noticed that most successful sign companies were run by a team of two—two brothers, two sisters, or two spouses. Four years after buying Miramar, after their two sons were older, his wife, Karen Sypolt, joined as the head of sales. Her experience selling office furniture helped the company enormously, he said, and was key in getting them through the recession.

After some initial tension, they learned the importance of defining their roles and responsibilities and trusting that the other person would make the appropriate decision. He handles the back office, and she is the major link with customers—and they are still happily married.

The hardest part of owning Miramar has been "managing the 100 holes in the dike. Every sign is unique, and we are making something different every day," said Jester. As a small-business owner, you are always responsible, and it's hard to take time off.

Today, the company has 12 employees and posted revenue in 2012 of $1.2 million, according to Jester, who expects sales will rise to $1.35 million this year.

(Neil's note: I love the idea that Paul morphed from high-tech software [HNC] to low-tech American manufacturing; he makes real things.)

Jester and Sypolt have never looked back and believe the rewards of business ownership are about more than money. The benefits include being able to hire their sons in order to teach them about business and to set the corporate culture and rules (they love bringing their dogs to work).

During his career in corporations, Jester grew to hate meetings, so Miramar holds very few of them. Most importantly, he said, "I'm truly the captain of my ship, I love my team, and ownership is addictive and satisfying."

DEALING WITH ANXIETY IN NO UNCERTAIN TERMS
November 11, 2013

Rule #12:
The entrepreneur needs to not only tolerate ambiguity;
he needs to embrace it.

What is the correlation between ambiguity and anxiety? It turns out other people have wondered about this, namely Harvard Business School professor Alison Wood Brooks.

In the recent article "Overcoming Nervous Nelly," in *Harvard Business School Working Knowledge*, she posits that at its core, "anxiety is about uncertainty"—the worry associated with what "might" happen rather than something that will likely happen. Remember your mother's advice, "Don't cross the bridge until you get to it." What you, the entrepreneur, feel, is that you do not have control over the events, and this out-of-control feeling can cause deep anxiety.

So, how does anxiety manifest itself and cause poor negotiation outcomes? One common expression is talking too soon; one has to learn to tolerate the silence. Another is an early lowball offer because you fear the other person will walk away. Barbara and I experience this in our class when we discuss "pre-money valuation." The entrepreneur picks a number out of relatively thin air and then gets nervous when the investor just stares—and begins to chuckle.

Anxiety also can express itself in the need to surround yourself with advisers. It is rational to seek advice from so-called experts, but if you are in a state of high anxiety, you won't know a good adviser from a bad one and good advice from bad advice. Your powers of perception are impacted negatively because you are uncomfortable. The trick for the entrepreneur is to know which adviser is really going to give you the really good advice. Even worse, Brooks found that a substantial number of advisers take advantage of their clients' anxiety to increase their own profits. This one is easy—just repeat the words financial adviser, wealth manager and stockbroker. Not all of them, but enough to keep the feds busy suing a bunch of them.

My father had a maxim: "When you don't know what to do, do nothing." It is actually rational to embrace the anxiety and then allow it to subside by virtue of increased self-awareness and information—the more you know, the less you feel vulnerable. Think of the negotiation for a car when you are armed with the MSRP and the manufacturer's rebate.

Another way to deal with anxiety is to create rituals. For example, some professional tennis players bounce the ball anywhere from eight to 18 times before they serve. This calms them down and makes their opponent nuts. Rituals work. When I fly, during takeoff I have a secret handshake with myself. Don't laugh. It has worked fine so far.

Another technique that Brooks suggests is to "turn anxiety into excitement." If you say, "I am excited about" rather than saying "Be calm," it dramatically changes the outcome of your performance. She advocates combining high arousal with a sense of excitement.

A confession: I play golf, and I often approach a difficult shot with the words, "Here is an opportunity for greatness." While it has on occasion proven true, I am not leaving my job to go on the PGA's senior tour. However, Brooks statistically proves that combining "excitement" with your anxiety leads to more positive outcomes. Positive thinking creates positive outcomes and allows you to better embrace ambiguity.

So now we come to ambiguity. I think a key element for entrepreneurial success is the willingness to be comfortable without all the answers—to be willing to imagine success rather than fear the consequences of failure.

And that leads to considering, "What is the worst thing that can happen?" Yes, failure is always an option, if not, in fact, a likelihood. So every time you start a project, remember this: The worst thing that can happen is that you will fail—but you are probably not going to drop dead. Which means you have a chance to do it all over again.

DON'T DISCOUNT THE ROLE THAT LUCK AND CHANCE PLAY IN BUSINESS LIFE

October 14, 2013

"Do I feel lucky? Well, do ya, punk?" is one of the iconic lines from American cinema. The movie is *Dirty Harry*, and the actor is Clint Eastwood. How does luck and chance fit into the life of the entrepreneur? How do you know when opportunity has shown up and you need to take advantage of it now?

I just finished reading Billy Crystal's new book, *Still Fooling 'Em*, and there is a moment that happens by chance early in Billy's life. Jack Rollins, the most famous manager of comedians, happens to see his act at the comedy club Catch a Rising Star. Rollins criticizes the act and offers some strong suggestions. Billy listens and makes the adjustments. Rollins takes him on and, as they say, the rest is history.

I recently watched an episode of *Shark Tank* in which the contestant was pitching some kind of goofy idea. Mark Cuban showed some interest while the other sharks had all passed. The contestant wanted $300,000, for which he was offering 10 percent of the company. Clearly, this is an insane valuation. Cuban countered with "I am interested. What will you give me for $350,000?" The contestant mumbled and fumbled and finally told Cuban that his professor/partner thinks the valuation is fair. Then he begrudgingly offered to increase the deal to 15 percent. Cuban promptly passed. Game over.

The contestant walked out, turned to the camera and said, "Wow, I can't believe I just turned down Mark Cuban." Neither could I. If you can get Mark Cuban to give you both time and money, you take it. The valuation is meaningless. The right answer would have been, "Mr. Cuban, what percent ownership would you like?"

I believe chance and luck are not random. They do show up in your life. They are like a sine wave. They come and go; they have a rhythm. My favorite author, Daniel Kahneman, says they are like a train that periodically comes through the station. If you happen to be standing on the platform, get on the train.

In my own life, there are countless stories of chance and luck playing enormous roles. I found the money for a downtown high-rise condominium by standing in the pasta salad line. (Full story in my book).

The assignment for the entrepreneur is to recognize it when it shows up and to seize it. But how do you differentiate the Mark Cubans from the Joe Schmos? And how do you maximize the opportunity to be standing on the platform when the "luck train" roars by?

Unfortunately, the maxim "It's not what you know, but who you know that matters," is still true.

A young entrepreneur came to see me, and I referred her to my partner, who has the most connected Rolodex this side of Mark Andreessen. They met and unfortunately were not able to make a deal. The entrepreneur was being asked to give up a piece of her company, but it was structured as pay-for-performance—no money raised, no ownership created.

This model is somewhat different from the typical "adviser" who gets a couple points for giving advice and maybe helping out. It is always awkward to carve those points back, even when you find the adviser to be a semi-charlatan and not particularly effective. The entrepreneur had a medical device company, and my partner knows members of the board of Johnson & Johnson. This deal should have been a no-brainer.

In fairness, the entrepreneur needs to road test the adviser before committing to a relationship, and the adviser should get nothing without demonstrated performance.

Still, the hard part for the entrepreneur is how to find the Rolodex—the real value-add—the Mark Cuban, the Jack Rollins effect—the person or team that can provide the rocket fuel for launch. And to maximize the chance for chance to arrive, you need to hang around the train station and be very flexible, open to negotiation and renegotiation, talk to everyone, including the porter and the baggage handler (you never know), be humble, but also opportunistic—and then when the Super Chief comes roaring through—jump on.

Rule #324:
All aboard.

RUNNING FOOD TRUCKS NO EASY RIDE
March 12, 2013

In 1866, Charles Goodnight, a cattle herder, invented the chuck wagon. In 1890, lunch wagons came to New York City to feed the workers on the night shift. In the 1950s, the Army got into the game with mobile canteens.

In 2013, the world has moved from roach coaches to gourmet food on wheels, geo-located on your smartphone and serving high-end specialty food, and people line up when they know it is arriving. The iron chef meets meals on wheels. The only thing missing is the jingle from the old-fashioned ice cream truck.

One of our favorite rules—#218: Relentless pursuit and grand passion will take you further than good grades—is particularly applicable to this business, which sounds glamorous from the outside but requires long hours and perseverance in order to be successful.

Marko Pavlinovic, owner of Mangia Mangia Mobile, usually works six days a week, 14 hours a day. On a recent Thursday, he started cooking at 6 a.m. at the Kearny Mesa commercial kitchen where he rents space. At 9:45 a.m., he left for MCAS Miramar, where he served Italian specialties such as spaghetti and meatballs and chicken parmigiana sandwiches from 10:30 a.m. to 3 p.m. Then he headed back to the kitchen to load up more food and drinks for his dinner stop from 5 to 8 p.m. The day ended with scrubbing pots and pans and cleaning the truck.

In 2002, Pavlinovic came to San Diego from Italy on vacation. He ended up getting a work permit and a job as a waiter. Two years ago, he started Mangia Mangia Mobile because he wanted to translate his love of food into a business. His mother and grandmother provided the recipes, and the initial capital was $16,000 in savings. He tried and failed to get a bank loan, so he rented a truck for $2,000 a month. By the time that he had paid the truck owner three months of rent in advance, made some interior modifications, painted the truck, purchased pots and pans, insurance and food, he had $350 left on the day that he opened.

In his second week of business, the Cooking Channel asked a well-known food blogger to identify the best food truck in San Diego. She recommended Mangia Mangia. "When they called, they said this is the Cooking Channel, do you want to be on TV? I hung up the phone because I thought that a friend was fooling me," he said.

The segment aired eight months later, and his business has grown steadily since then.

Last year, he purchased his own truck with a $35,000 loan from Accion, a nonprofit lender that makes small-business loans between $300 and $35,000. A growing part of his business is catering, and future plans are to sell packaged items such as his asparagus lasagna at farmers' markets and in local stores.

Like Pavlinovic, Jennifer and Chris Saint couldn't get a bank loan when they started Sweet Treats Truck five years ago. Jennifer had been a residential real estate broker, and Christ, her husband, was a private investigator before he was disabled from a spinal cord tumor.

The Saints purchased a used truck with a $35,000 Accion loan that they have repaid. With their profits and a $30,000 loan from Certified Development Corp., they bought a second truck, so now they have one for ice cream and one for other desserts.

Sometimes your first approach doesn't work, and then comes the infamous pivot. "Our original thought was to cater to people getting out of bars at 2 a.m., but then we found out that drunk people don't eat ice cream," said Jennifer. Their new focus became corporate events, and they have been profitable since their second year.

Unlike most other food trucks, the Saints do not make the products that they sell.

"We want to support other local small businesses and get their product out to the street," Jennifer said.

With all the attention on celebrity chefs, more people are getting into the gourmet food truck business. When the Saints started, Jennifer said there were only a handful in San Diego, and now there are more than 60. But it is a tough gig, and trucks come and go, giving truth to the old saying, "If you can't take the heat, get out of the kitchen."

ENTREPRENEURS SHOULD REMEMBER FIVE STAGES OF GRIEF

October 7, 2013

Rule #3:
You just think it is the end of the world.
Trust me, that is at least two to three more companies
off in the future.

When an entrepreneur asks me to serve as a mentor, the assumption that both parties make is that we are working together to build, grow, and manage the early-stage company for success. But I am beginning to wonder if perhaps a different kind of mentoring experience might also be useful—one that helps the entrepreneur manage and deal with failure.

Elisabeth Kübler-Ross is famous for defining "the five stages of grief." These are denial, anger, bargaining, depression, and acceptance. (Lenny Bruce has a famous performance on this topic that you can find online.) Entrepreneurs in failing companies go through these same stages.

- Denial: I have seen entrepreneurs continue on, blindly, fueled by the mantra and belief that an entrepreneur needs "passion" for his project. "If I can raise another small round and get a few more downloads." This chant is oblivious to the fact that maybe no one wants it. It is the famous joke about the man who jumps off the Empire State Building. As he passes the 46th floor, a man at the window shouts out, "How are you doing?" and the jumper answers, "So far, so good." A good failure mentor is needed to point out the concrete below.

- Anger: Why me? All those half-baked companies that obtain financing at crazy valuations. This becomes the "why not me" version of anger. Now, this person offers an interesting case because it is wholly possible that their company is actually terrific and the fact that some venture capitalist somewhere barfed on them is not necessarily indicative of the merit of the company. But again, the failure mentor has to act in a way that honors the anger but does not allow it to enter the realm of rage and self-destructive behavior. Look, I have been passed over for things that I felt I deserved. My answer is a simple one—revenge. The "I will show those half-wits" anger and so I go back to work with even more purpose.

- Bargaining: This entrepreneur says, "I will do anything if you will give me more time, more money"—more, more, more. This entrepreneur is dangerous for the investor because you can make a great deal, but be careful. I am not sure I want to be a contributor to the human train wreck that is coming down the tracks. So the failure mentor needs to preach acceptance—preparation for the end that is looming.

- Depression: This feeling is real. A young friend recently asked me, "If my company fails, I will probably end up homeless living out of a garbage bin." When you live by comparison, when you look around you and your friends are getting married, having children, buying houses, and getting paid outrageous sums of money, feeling depressed may actually be perfectly reasonable. The failure mentor needs to refer our friend to a shrink who can prescribe meds.

- Acceptance: The ultimate state of Zen. I acknowledge reality, and I am at peace. Now, look, that sounds great, but I do not want to fund an entrepreneur who is accepting. I am more of the anger and rage school. The key to acceptance is the recognition that it is not the end, it is not death. In fact, acceptance is wonderful because like a divorce or a bankruptcy or a failure, you are free to get up and try to do better the next time. What is important is accepting the current reality and letting go of the past. The failure mentor's job here is to encourage our entrepreneur to analyze the failure, really wallow in it, dig deep into the issues—not just the business, but the psychological, the personal, to do the hard look in the mirror—and to come out the other side ready to crush the ball the next time.

BEING A "GIVER," NOT A "TAKER," IS GOOD FOR BUSINESS

February 10, 2014

One of my business partners is a "giver," and in an effort to enhance and improve his partner, he gave me a book, appropriately titled *Give and Take*, by Adam Grant. While our column is not normally the *New York Review of Books*, this week I'm going to go rogue and tell you about this book and how it can change your life.

The book's premise is simple. Traditionally, the entrepreneurial drivers to success have been passion, hard work, talent, dedication, and luck. But Grant argues (and proves) that success is increasingly dependent on how we interact with others. In other words, success hinges more on effective networking, collaboration, influence, negotiation, and leadership—all of which are informed by and made more valuable by being a "giver."

Grant posits that there are three kinds of people in the world: "takers," "matchers," and "givers." We all know what a taker is—scorched earth, sort of what's mine is mine and what's yours is mine. A taker is always thinking "what can you do for me?" rather than "what can I do for you?"

Matchers are slightly more evolved. They have an internal balance mechanism that measures giving and taking—recognizing the basic principle of win-win, but always measuring. They know clearly when they are not being reciprocated.

And then there are givers. This is the enlightened species that provides service, guidance, care, feeding, and comfort without any immediate expectation of recompense or match or equality. The giver is someone who has an internal desire to genuinely share. Now before you chuckle at the naiveté of being a giver, the book also explains how to be a giver without being a schmuck. The giver comes from a position of power, not weakness.

Grant profiles famous television writer George Meyer, of *The Simpsons*, who wrote a large number of the shows but took much less credit than he was entitled to. His behavior, talent, and generosity energized and inspired the rest of the writing staff and made the show even better.

He also profiles David Hornik of August Capital. In the rotten, competitive world of the venture capitalist, Hornik stands like a beacon on the hill of helping others, often initially at his own expense—and then like the true giver, deals and success come back to him in a tsunami.

Grant also writes about Stu Inman, a basketball coach who sometimes "stayed too long" with his draft choices, and yet, once again, at the end, was enormously successful.

Another example is Adam Rifkin, who in 2011 had more LinkedIn connections to the 640 powerful people on *Fortune*'s list than any human being on the planet. And you probably have not heard of him. Rifkin's maxim is "I believe in the strength of weak ties." It turns out that acquaintances are more important in the networking ecosystem than strong, close friends.

Herewith a quote from a man some would consider a world-class taker, Bill Gates. "There are two great forces of human nature—self-interest and caring for others," and it is proven that people are the most successful when they develop a hybrid engine, mixing the two fuels. He gets it.

Successful givers are "otherish." They are ambitious in their own goals and equally and simultaneously care about benefiting others.

I love this paradox. In our own little entrepreneurial ecosystem in San Diego, we all have met the trio—takers, matchers, and givers. Now, here is the puzzler for the founder seeking assistance as well as the seasoned executive—how to pick your mentor, who should I invest time in?

I have my own rule about negotiation. If I have the upper hand and if I make a deal "too good" for me, I will often go back the next day and renegotiate against myself. I feel the obligation to protect the other person when it is not a fair fight. When I have all the guns and all the ammo, I know that I can avoid war, not by keeping all the weapons, but in fact by giving a few of them back to the other guy. If you want confirmation on that one, read Grant's chapter about Derek Sorenson.

Give and Take is a monster book. It will change your life. I am now more committed to increasing my "giver" quotient. Because I know I will like myself better, and on top of that, it's good business.

NEGOTIATION REQUIRES A BIT OF IMPROVISATION, LIKE IN JAZZ

May 12, 2014

"And all that jazz."

This lyric is from *Chicago*, one of the best musicals of all time and winner of six Tony Awards. A couple of weeks ago, Barbara and I attended a jazz concert where we heard John Pizzarelli and Ramsey Lewis—and wow.

What fascinated me was the fact that they sort of made it up as they went along. Jazz is all about improvisation—listening to the other musicians, heading out on your own riff, and then surfing back into the mainstream, and then another musician picks it up and sets out again.

Recently, the *Harvard Business Review* published an article, "Negotiation and All that Jazz," by Michael Wheeler, a retired Harvard Business School professor. He suggests (a bit tongue in cheek) that if you want to win at negotiating, you should maybe learn to play an instrument.

He quotes Gen. Dwight Eisenhower: "Plans go out the window at the first contact with the enemy—plans, per se, are worthless." But then Eisenhower adds the kicker: "But planning is everything."

So the connection between jazz, improvisation, and negotiation is an interesting one. Assuming the other side is equal in skills and determination, then falling back only on the two mainstream models—win-win or scorched earth—will not be enough to prevail.

You need to take a lesson from another master negotiator, Alonzo "Jake" Gaither, head coach at Florida A&M from 1945 to 1969. His famous quote: "I want my boys to be agile, mobile, and hostile." That strikes me as a good opening stance. (Easy on the hostile, at least until the other side brings out an AK-47.)

Wheeler says, "Negotiation entails ongoing learning, adapting, and influencing," which are clearly the exact elements in a great jazz rendition. He goes on: "Negotiation is like dancing on a tabletop in the pitch dark. You need to embrace chaos." Chaos theory studies the behavior of dynamical systems that are sensitive to initial conditions—sometimes referred to as the "butterfly effect." (If only I had listened to my mother and stayed with the piano lessons . . .)

Wheeler quotes Richard Holbrooke, a famous diplomat: "It's improvisation on a theme (jazz)—you know where you want to go, but you don't know how to get there." (If only someone would invent GPS for negotiation.)

Great jazz musicians listen as well as they play. They suspend judgment, they wait their turn, and when they begin to play they "complement" the tune—they are not discordant—they look for mutuality of the sound, they play off and improve, but at the same time, they also nudge the other musicians in a certain direction.

The jazz artist "works with what he is given." He can't start over, he can't bend it in a "predetermined" direction.

Even though the late Steve Jobs, Apple's co-founder, had a force field to bend reality, most of us mortals can't do that. We need to adapt our initial blueprint to reality, not the other way around.

And finally, it is OK to be anxious, to be unresolved, to not only tolerate ambiguity, but to embrace it. You are not the master of your ship even though you may have paid for it. There are things such as wind and waves. And in the negotiation game, a successful outcome is never assured. Even worse, after it ends, and you think you have won, you begin to wonder.

Wheeler talks about "staying in the game." The idea here is to be both simultaneously calm and alert, open to the process of discovery.

Tom Green, who crafted a $350 billion health-care settlement with the tobacco industry in the late 1990s, says the secret to his success is "making chaos my friend in negotiation."

Jazz is chaotic but also structured and rational. If all else fails, the next time I have to go to the mat on a deal, I am going to bring in a bass fiddle, and if I'm asked if I can play it, I will say no—and then just smash it over the head of the other person. Music to my ears.

Rule #353:
Listen to the sounds between the notes.
They are the music.

CLOSING DEAL WITH INVESTOR TAKES PRACTICE, POKER FACE

September 11, 2012

A few weeks ago, I helped a friend refinance his underwater home mortgage. For a number of reasons, I was intimately involved (I needed to cosign), and as you can imagine, it was a miserable experience. Nothing new there.

It got me thinking about what it means "to close," meaning to bring a deal to a successful conclusion. This skill is essential and critical to the entrepreneur, and most importantly, it can be learned.

Recently, I assisted in the sale of a business. It required obtaining 37 signatures from past employees and minor stockholders, most of whom had dispersed to the ends of the earth. The process took nine weeks, and the company founder literally flew to Boston to get the last two. Relentless pursuit won the day on that one.

Now, here is what happened with the home mortgage refinance fiasco. It required threatening, cajoling, begging, drawing a line in the sand, and finally making an adjustment at the last minute to get the deal done. One would like to believe that rational people would act in their own economic best self-interest. That is not necessarily the case.

The whole refinance game is insane. The only way you can get the bank to accommodate a reasoned request is to act badly—to stop paying the mortgage. If you are current and call up and say, "Let's make a deal," they say, "Why should we? You are still paying the mortgage." Then you stop paying and 12 to 20 months later they say, "OK, let's make a deal." You achieve the desired result, but only by acting badly. This is crazy.

Let's look at venture/angel financing. The investor is interested. He says send me more stuff, it seems like a good deal, but could we see some more information, and then we would like to discuss it with our partners, we will get back to you, until you say, "We are closing in nine days. Are you in or out?"

Note to entrepreneur: You need to learn to say that with a straight face, even though you do not have any money in the bank, and there is no one else who will fund you. Practice this in front of a mirror without laughing.

The goal is to create a sense of urgency and scarcity.

And then there are the lawyers. They can be friend or foe in getting a deal closed. Their job is to make sure there are no loose ends. And there are always loose ends. You need to manage their lawyers—not necessarily yours. Do not let them open new items at the final bell. Tell them, "We are closing in nine days or we are walking."

Now I recognize this is easy to say and hard to do. This thing called "closing" is not technical, it does not lend itself to an algorithm, and it is not taught in any MBA classroom. There is no formula. Its components are different every time. It has elements of game theory, but when it is your deal (and your only deal), it is not theory.

Having said the above, I need to provide a bit of caution. It reminds me of those car commercials where some guy is driving 180 miles per hour on a rain-soaked street and then does a 360-degree turn and parallel parks in a space just big enough for a baby's stroller. At the bottom of the screen, it says, "professional driver, do not try this at home."

Learning how to close is a skill. It comes from experience—much like the professional driver who has learned to turn a car on a rain-soaked street.

Simply being at the table and telling the other guy "take it or leave it" without having done the prep work is a recipe for disaster.

Closing is the whole game. It is when the points are put on the board. It is all about relentless pursuit, and the awareness that the other side can only see its own cards.

Rule #128:
No deal is perfect,
but some deals are more perfect than others.

TAKING OUR KNOWLEDGE TO A CAPTIVE AUDIENCE
June 2, 2014

My book, *I'm There for You Baby*, contains 231 rules for entrepreneurial success, and the first one is the most important. It says, "Return every email and every phone call."

Recently out of the blue, I got an email that floored me. Here is an excerpt:

"My boyfriend is currently incarcerated at the Consolidated Brig at Miramar . . . He is brainstorming several ideas post incarceration . . . Would you be interested in possibly teaching a course at the Brig?"

Come on, you can't make this stuff up, and you cannot say no to that one.

And so began my continuing education. First off, Miramar is a very big place, and finding the right person was the first problem. Meet Michelle Davis, M.S., Offender Workforce Development Specialist. She is in charge of re-entry and transition. She wrote to me, "All (of the inmates) are looking for hope, inspiration, resources, and guidance before taking the next journey in their lives."

I am embarrassed to admit that I have never even thought about soldiers and the problem of re-entry, let alone prisoners. Barbara and I have taught our entrepreneurship class at UCSD for several years, and mostly our students are Ph.D. candidates in neuro, bio, computer science, nano, etc.—bright students with an excellent education and opportunities for entrepreneurial success. But now I was going to get a chance to meet some very different students—perhaps a bit less advantaged, but no less desirous of thinking about entrepreneurship. I did ask Davis what to call the attendees in my session. Her answer? "We call them prisoners." Clearly, I had a lot to learn.

This column was written before I went to the brig, and next week's column will be about my experiences. An important part of the story is "Marcia"—the woman with the boyfriend who wrote to Barbara and me.

She is 26, the youngest of six children and grew up in Los Angeles. She said that her father was "murdered on the streets of Los Angeles" when she was 19. She graduated from Cal State San Marcos, where she competed in track and field and held multiple jobs to pay for college.

While in San Diego, she met a marine, "Steve," and they fell in love. He was caught dealing drugs, and he has 10 months left to serve in the brig. An old story, but Marcia has big plans. She is passionate about making the world a better place. She has overcome a multitude of challenges, and she is committed to helping people "unleash their inner child" and fulfill their dreams.

So how did she get to Barbara and me? Well, it seems that *U-T San Diego* is distributed to the prisoners, and her boyfriend is an avid reader of our column. And Steve suggested to Marcia that she reach out to us. A blind ask.

But, let's go back to Davis. In her email to us, she wrote, "Most individuals will have challenging criminal records and punitive discharges, but they want to talk about entrepreneurship." Everyone wants to take charge of their life, to be reinvented, re-imagined, and I guess in some way, reborn. And I intend to try hard to meet that test at Miramar.

After all, our little angel investment company is called Blackbird Ventures. The name was inspired by the movie, *The Maltese Falcon*. In the final scene, the local gumshoe asks Humphrey Bogart, who is holding the heavy bird, just what this black dingus is anyway, and Bogart says, "It's the stuff that dreams are made of."

It is the stuff of entrepreneurship—the hunt, the search, the adventure, the lust, the revenge—and of course, yes, always, the girl. (In my case I did get Barbara Bry, so on that score, I won.)

Next week, I will share the story of Steve and my captive audience.

GIVING ENTREPRENEURIAL GUIDANCE TO OUR TROOPS IN THE BRIG

June 9 2014

Except for the fact that the men and women were dressed in fatigues, they looked like one of our classes at UCSD.

Eighty prisoners (25 percent of whom were women) were seated in last month's class at the brig at Marine Corps Air Station Miramar in San Diego, eager to listen to some thoughts on entrepreneurship, reinvention, and renewal, as they anticipated re-entering regular society.

What was thrilling was their palpable desire to learn something about business.

Now some of my "students" already knew something about business. A few had been active in drug trafficking where the margins are high, the product demand is deep, the market is unlimited, there is price elasticity, and you can get a customer for life. Unfortunately that business is also illegal, so I suggested they consider applying the same basic business principles to an opportunity where they would not end up in jail or dead. There were smiles. This group was cool.

During the Vietnam era, I was a member of the armed services, and I pointed out that they already knew a lot about teams, about determination, about discipline, about integrity and courage.

In fact, the military is an outstanding training ground for entrepreneurship. These young men and women were already in the problem-solving business. I tried to remind them that what they had learned as soldiers were exactly the characteristics necessary to succeed in any business adventure.

I showed them an introductory PowerPoint presentation—the same one I show to the students in our UC San Diego class. I did not dumb it down. And their questions were the same as I have heard before.

I challenged them with the "rich vs. king" puzzle, and they instinctively got it right. There are no kings in the military.

One young lady broke my heart when she said, "I don't want to be rich or king, I want to make a difference." Wow.

They asked about franchises vs. starting from scratch. And they were deeply hungry for mentors. Certainly Score San Diego is one such resource, but I am ashamed to tell you that I had never really focused on the magnitude of the problem that the "re-entry-into-society soldier" faces. And many of these men and women will re-enter with a dishonorable discharge. You try to explain that to a potential employer.

They asked about co-founders (I feel strongly about the importance of having one), and I told them to find someone with complementary skills. Your company probably does not need two demolition experts.

So here comes the ask. They begged me for reading material, for business books, for management books, for leadership books—for anything that could give them some entrepreneurial guidance. They were hungry for education in this area.

The military has rules. It cannot accept donations, so you cannot send money.

So, I have picked out seven books—*The Black Swan*, *The Lean Startup*, *The Hard Thing about Hard Things*, *Thinking, Fast and Slow*, *Crossing the Chasm*, *The Art of the Start*, and *Getting to Plan B*. I am buying several copies of each and sending them to the brig.

I am going to ask our readers to do something similar.

Please either send copies of those books or send copies of any business book that has been important to you, that has elevated or inspired your thinking.

As I mentioned previously, this is a captive audience with time to read and study. Currently, 300 prisoners are in the Miramar Brig. You do the math.

You can send the books (no money) to Michelle V. Davis, Re-entry Coordinator, Offender Workforce Development Specialist, Naval Consolidated Brig Miramar, 46141 Miramar Way, San Diego, CA 92145.

Rule #1:
Return every email and every phone call.

THE BEST BUSINESS BOOKS EXPAND YOUR THINKING
October 9, 2012

"The business of business is business," said the Nobel Prize-winning economist Milton Friedman. And selling books about business is one of those very big businesses. Giving business advice is a national pastime, and one needs to beware of the famous syndrome, "Those who can, do, and those who can't, teach (or write books)"—and yours truly is guilty as charged on both counts.

While you may find some interesting information in books that offer seven principles on how to raise money or 10 ways to market your product, we believe the true value of great business books is in their ability to expand your thinking—to create a unique environment for intellectual wrestling—whether you own a bakery or a biotech.

Here are a few of our favorites:

- Two books by Daniel Kahneman top our list. *Choices, Values and Frames*, co-authored by Amos Tversky, tackles one of our favorite topics—the importance of rational behavior and how to embrace it. It expands on one of our favorite rules—#302: More money is lost through neurotic behavior than through bad business decisions. We also like Kahneman's newest book, *Thinking, Fast and Slow*, which is a counterpoint to *Blink* by Malcolm Gladwell, a good book but not on our top list. In *Thinking, Fast and Slow*, Kahneman explores what he calls System 1 and System 2 thinking, and it has made us re-examine how we make decisions and whether we too often jump to conclusions.

- Originally published in 1991, *Crossing the Chasm* by Geoffrey Moore is still relevant today because marketing is often the area in which entrepreneurs run into problems. They build a "cool" product that they like but they have no idea whether it fills a customer need or how to persuade anyone to buy it. In *Crossing the Chasm*, Moore explores techniques on how to first attract innovators and early adopters and then move across the chasm to what he calls the early majority, late majority and laggards.

- *Steve Jobs* by Walter Isaacson is the best biography that we've read in the last five years. While none of us is Steve Jobs, we can learn a lot from the journey that he and Apple traveled. It is revealing to read how a man and a company changed not only an industry but an entire culture. We were intrigued by Jobs' famous "reality distortion field" that allowed him to push the boundaries beyond what most people thought possible. Yet, this trait that made Jobs so successful in business may have cost him years off his life because he thought that he could "will" his disease away, rather than seek medical treatment.

- *The Black Swan* by Nassim Nicholas Taleb is Neil's favorite and it puts into perspective Rule #217, "It's what you don't know that you don't know that will kill you." A "black swan" is an extremely unlikely event, positive or negative, that has major repercussions.

- *The Innovator's Dilemma* by Clayton M. Christensen focuses on disruptive technology and why successful companies often lose their market leadership or go out of business completely when new technologies emerge. Think about what happened to horse and buggy manufacturers when automobiles came along, typewriter companies when personal computers came along or record retailers when iTunes came along. An entrepreneur has to continually address the environment, the competition and new technologies. Large companies often have a hard time jettisoning existing business lines—which of course creates an opportunity for the entrepreneur.

- We loved *The Secret Life of Houdini: The Making of America's First Superhero* by William Kalush because Houdini was a master at reinventing himself over and over again—traits important in entrepreneurship. Also, entrepreneurship is a little bit like holding your breath under water. You don't think that you can do it any longer, and then you find out that you can.

- Neil recommends *The Catcher in the Rye* by J.D. Salinger, which he first read in the 10th grade. He recalls, "The teacher was telling us what the book meant. I was sitting in the back of the class, and I told him that he had misinterpreted everything, that he had it all wrong. He asked me how I could be so sure. I told him that I knew he was wrong, because I was Holden Caulfield, whereupon, he tossed me out of the class. But I got the last laugh—I actually know where the ducks go in winter."

WHO WOULD YOU DEEM WORTHY OF A SECOND CHANCE?

February 2, 2015

"Gimme a second chance."

I went back to the Miramar brig last month (third time, but I don't have to stay overnight) to talk to about 70 inmates on the subject of entrepreneurship. The topic this time was the "20 reasons Startups Fail." If you regularly read this column, you already know them by heart—team, market, money, etc.

But when it came time for questions, I got one that stopped me in my tracks. "Would you hire a convicted felon?" Whoa. Real world here, wake up, pay attention.

I told them that the issue was not the crime per se, but if you failed to disclose the issue early in the interview process, and if it were found out later, that probably would kill your chances. Transparency is the order of the day. At the same time, the crimes that these men and women were in the brig for were not on the order of murder and mayhem. They were primarily disciplinary and drug related.

And to compound the complexity, I would argue that former military are often the very best people to hire. The issues of team, discipline, goals—those are instilled in the military. We all know about programs to support hiring a veteran, and I would argue that is not doing someone a favor—that, in fact, a veteran brings huge skills.

But the question hung in the air. I wondered if we as a society discriminate against gender, against race, against sexual orientation—and then to top it off, do we give second chances to people who have made a criminal mistake? It is easy to pay lip service, but do we really give second chances?

So now let's look at second chances for entrepreneurs. Here is a statistic that will chill your bones a bit. Harvard did a study on failure, and here is what Shikhar Ghosh found: "If failure means the investors lose most of their money, the rate is 30 to 40 percent. If it means that the startup did not achieve the anticipated financial return, the rate is 70 to 80 percent. nd if failure is defined as falling short of projections, the rate is 90 to 95 percent."

In the entrepreneurship game, "failure" is a badge of honor to be worn proudly and serves you well when you do the next company. And many things outside your control—timing, market, money, demand, customer, revenue, etc.—often affect that failure.

But one of the biggest problems, says Ghosh, is too much money, not too little. "When you don't have money, you reformulate the dog food so that the dogs will eat it. When you have a lot of money, you can afford to argue with the dogs that it is nutritious and good for them and they should like it."

The venture community values experience over a clean slate. Henry Ford, Steve Jobs, and Gururaj "Desh" Deshpande all experienced multiple failures before achieving success.

But Ghosh also warns about personal failures. Those are when the individual does something that violates a fiduciary duty, commits a crime or is immoral. And personal failures often come when the CEO is trying desperately to save his company and he crosses the line, he misrepresents, he commits fraud. Ghosh says that when you do that, you are taking an enterprise failure and making it a personal failure—and that is not easily forgiven.

Back to the Naval Consolidated Brig. My students had each committed some kind of personal failure, but I think as a society we need to find generosity and give second chances. Stuff happens. I believe in redemption; every failed entrepreneur seeks it. Why should it be denied to others?

(Watch the final scene of the *Pulp Fiction* movie.)

The irony is that the financial world (Wall Street) hires the fallen back frequently, but the venture world appears to be less forgiving.

How will those of us who run companies respond when the candidate in front of you says that he or she has a criminal record?

Rule #387:
Walk a mile in someone else's shoes.
Your feet will hurt.

IN CONCLUSION

There is no conclusion. Entrepreneurship is an arc that extends to the ends of one's imagination, to the ends of the universe of possibilities. We all would like to wrap things up in a nice small blue box with a ribbon (I like to get Ms. Bry an occasional bauble from Tiffany's) but the world doesn't work that way.

There are moments of calm—moments when the world is spinning at exactly the right speed for your life, your company, your partner, your children—and then there is a small puff of wind, and the world starts to wobble on its axis and yes, sure enough, things begin to spin out of control again. But you had a moment, you had an instant when it was perfect. And the quest is to try to get the top to spin exactly correctly—again. And again. The process is never ending, and the top always wobbles in the end.

We all want to exert control, and that is not possible—at least not for long periods of time. You get a fraction of a moment. You need to embrace the moment, acknowledge the wonder of a perfectly spinning top, and know that moment will not last.

You continue on because you want to see if you can capture the moment again. What's important is that winning is self-defined. In the end, winning is just a moment like all the others. Then the top starts to wobble and you have to go back into the fray again to see if you can set it right—and even then, only for a moment.

Enjoy the moments and the journey.

—Neil Senturia

ACKNOWLDEGMENTS

Thank you to Jeff Light, Diana McCabe and Nirmala Bhat at the *San Diego Union-Tribune*; Cliff Boro; John and Janet McCulley; Karla Olson; Nicole Rockstead; and all the entrepreneurs who shared their stories.